Promises for
Dynamic Living

An 80 day reflective journey from doubt to assurance

Linda Knight

Copyright © 2015 by Linda Knight

Scripture quotations marked "NIV" are taken from the *Holy Bible, New International Version®. NIV®*. Copyright © 1973, 1978, 1984 by International Bible Society. Used by permission of Zondervan. All rights reserved.

Scripture quotations marked "ESV" are taken from *The Holy Bible, English Standard Version®* (ESV®). Copyright ©2001 by Crossway Bibles, a division of Good News Publishers. Used by permission. All rights reserved.

FIRST EDITION

ISBN: 978-0-9962716-3-9

Library of Congress Control Number: 2015943874

Published by

P.O. Box 2839, Apopka, FL 32704

Printed in the United States of America

Disclaimer: The views and opinions expressed in this book are solely those of the authors and other contributors. These views and opinions do not necessarily represent those of Certa Publishing.

Dedication

To my Bible Study Fellowship Sisters
who faithfully serve our LORD

and

To my Mom and Dad for their love and faith

*"His divine power has given us everything we need for life and godliness through our knowledge of him who called us by his own glory and goodness. Through these he has given us his **very great and precious promises**, so that through them you may participate in the divine nature and escape the corruption in the world caused by evil desires."*

2 Peter 1:3-4

Table of Contents

Days .... Promises Catagorized by Subjects .... Page

Accessibility of God

Christian Living

Courage

Faithfulness

Sovereignty

God's Word

Promises, Really Lord?

After I published my first book, *Fearless Living*, people asked me if I was going to write a second book. Since I never thought I would write even one book, I couldn't imagine God giving me a second one. However, while I was publishing my first book, God gave me a new idea to research. As I was studying the book of Genesis, I began to notice promises that God gave to Abraham that could apply to me. I started searching His Word for promises that I could claim in my own life. Each day, I would look up a new promise, write it in my journal, pray, and ask God what He was promising me through that particular verse. I saw His character revealed more and more and the vast scope of His promises. I became really excited about His promises, and what a difference I could see they were making in my life! I thought, I'm not the only one who needs to know the promises of God, nor am I the only one who needs His Word to penetrate in my life. Through His encouragement, *Promises for Dynamic Living* began to develop and become alive.

Knowing that pulling verses out of context could lead to error and misunderstanding, I searched God's Word to verify the chosen passages. Great promises of God are stated repeatedly in various contexts so that we can *get* the idea and claim the promise. Each day's devotional promise explains the truths we learn about God and where we can find a similar promise or concept in the Bible. I must admit, this search was a challenge and caused me to think, meditate, and internalize God's promises, as I saw them reaffirmed throughout His Word.

Through the writing of this book, I have seen the completeness of God's Word and how He has woven it together to confirm, assure, and build us up to be the men and women He desires. His Word in us glorifies Him, and He longs for us to study and know Him. When I work with young people, I try to teach them that God's Word, on the pages of our Bible, holds the same power as the spoken word of God, which brought the world into existence. There is power in His Word and He desires that we know His Word and claim it in our lives.

I am so encouraged because the depth of God's promises span throughout the entire Bible. God's promises are not just limited to those things given to us by Christ. God has been in the promise-making business from the very beginning of His relationship with man. He knows us and knows that we need assurance of who He is and what He will do in, and through, our lives. I pray you will find promises in both the Old and New Testaments to enrich your walk with the Lord and that it brings you assurance of His loving character. May His promises remove any, and all, doubts you are experiencing. Claiming His promises in your life will dispel doubt and fear. It will lead you on the pathway toward assurance and HOPE in Christ.

Blessings,

Linda

How To Use This Devotion

I know, from all the people I have talked to after writing *Fearless Living,* that there are many ways to approach a devotional. I have a friend that completed several days at one time, yet others completed the days with friends once a week. The *how* is not as important as the *doing.* So do what God leads you to do in order to get the most out of these days in your own life.

You could use each day as your daily devotion. Here are some steps to consider for getting the most out of your quiet time in God's Word:

- **Pray** before you begin each day and ask God for understanding.
- **Read** the selected promise and focus on what God is promising.
- **Look** at the listed "Lessons and Truths" about God and link them to the chosen promise.

- **Pray** the prayer.
- **Answer** the application questions and pray about them.
- **Search** the Scriptures for the "Promise Confirmation" verses, and think about how this adds to your knowledge of God and His purpose for you.

Other Ideas:

1. You could do one or two days a week, taking the time to memorize each day's Scripture. God encourages us to memorize His Word. Psalm 119:11 says, "I have hidden your word in my heart that I might not sin against you." God can use each of the promises to encourage and assure you. If you memorize them, the Holy Spirit can and will bring them in to remembrance when you need them the most.

2. You could do the days yourself and then join with a friend to challenge each other in the memorization of the verses. If you decide to memorize the Scriptures, use the "Promise Confirmation" verses as your study material for your daily devotions while you are working on memorization.

3. I have also included a "Subject Table of Contents" for the days. Each category could be a study by itself. You may be troubled by sin and in need of assurance of God's forgiveness. Looking at all the days that relate to forgiveness may help you better understand His forgiveness. It will allow you to come out from under the

burden of sin troubling you. Perhaps you want to be more courageous, focusing on 'courage' in God's promises will be reassuring and empowering.

Allow the Holy Spirit to guide you as delve into His Word. As for me, I am going to take the memorization challenge. I have some of the verses memorized, but there are many that I do not know. I find that there is a great benefit in learning these promises and knowing where they are located in the Bible. The hope and encouragement which memorizing these promises will bring me, will far exceed the time and energy I invest in learning. Memorizing Scripture has eternal value. Once you memorize a verse, it cannot be taken away from you. It will be with you for eternity.

I would love to hear from you, if you accept the challenge and endeavor to hide God's Word in your heart. Life is a constant challenge, and having God's Word in our minds, and hearts is a way for God to, constantly, assure and reassure us of His love and presence. 2 Timothy 3: 16-17 says, *"All Scripture is God-breathed and is useful for teaching, rebuking, correcting and training in righteousness so that the man of God may be thoroughly equipped for every good work."* Consider this promise as a way of God teaching and training you for His righteousness. To God be the glory for the great things He has done and great things He will do in—and through—us!

<u>Day 1</u>

God's Mercies

Lamentations 3:21-23

"*But this I call to mind, and therefore I have hope: The steadfast love of the LORD never ceases; his mercies never come to an end; they are new every morning; great is your faithfulness.*"

<u>Promise</u>: God promises His love and faithfulness will never end and His mercies are new each morning.

What encouragement do you need as you start this new study? God, in His mercy, gives us new hope every day. So many times, I get discouraged after experiencing a long and frustrating day, when things don't go well. Maybe I am struggling with relationships, troubling circumstances, health issues, or finances and at day's end I am in need of rest and refuge. God knows this and gives me this promise to assure me that each day will be a new beginning, and there is refreshed hope in Him.

<u>**Lessons and Truths**</u>:

1.   God is my source of HOPE.
2.   God's love is steadfast: firm, unswerving, constant, and resolute.
3.   His mercies are new each day and enough to supply all of my needs.
4.   God is faithful.

<u>Prayer</u>: Lord, you are, indeed, the Maker of each new day. You are sovereign and in control of *all* things. Give me hope in you and the ability to see your mercies, which come into my life each and every day. As I begin this study of your promises, help me to remember your faithfulness and to preserve a sense of wonder about the possibilities and assurances that you have for me in your Word. Amen.

<u>What is my response to God's promise?</u>

How am I depending on the love and mercy God is willing to provide for me?_______________________________________

____

____

When has God been faithful in the past, so that I know I can trust His faithfulness today? _________________________

____

Where do I need His mercies today? _________________

____

<u>Promise Confirmation</u>: Psalm 90:14, Isaiah 40:28-31, Jeremiah 29:11, Romans 8:38-39

<u>Day 2</u>

Resistance God's Way

James 4:7-8a

"*Submit yourselves therefore to God. Resist the devil, and he will flee from you. Draw near to God, and he will draw near to you.*"

<u>**Promise:**</u> God promises if I will *submit* (yield, obey) to Him, *resist* (oppose, withstand) Satan, and *come near* (approach) to Him, He will come near to me, and Satan will flee.

Claiming this promise requires that I submit, resist, and approach God. He is faithful and knows that Satan will stir up trouble in my life, *if* I let him. Scripture describes the Devil as a prowling, roaring lion (1 Peter 5:8). Yielding to God's way of living and standing firm against Satan's attacks is only achieved if I draw near to God. He promises that He is, and will always be, accessible to me. He *will* draw near to me and <u>Satan cannot reside where God does.</u> Praise God!

<u>**Lessons and Truths:**</u>

1. Obedience is God's way for me to fight and defeat Satan.
2. God is more powerful than Satan.
3. God is accessible and I can approach Him.
4. My nearness to God guarantees His nearness to me.

<u>**Prayer:**</u> Lord, give me a renewed spirit of obedience so that I may withstand Satan's attacks. I know that you will be with me and where you are Satan cannot abide. Hold me close, as I strive to live for you. Make me aware of my own stubbornness and resistance. Cover me with your grace so that I may live victoriously by your power. Amen.

<u>**What is my response to God's promise?**</u>

How am I submitting to God and following His Word? ______

____

____

Where am I lacking in my "resisting skills" because of my stubbornness and disobedience? ____________________

____

____

What can I do to experience God's nearness more clearly? __

____

____

<u>**Promise Confirmation**</u>: 1 Samuel 15:22, Psalm 1:1-3, Psalm 15, Hebrews 4:16, 1 Peter 5:8-9

<u>Day 3</u>

God's Pathway

Psalm 119:105

"Your word is a lamp to my feet and a light to my path."

<u>Promise</u>: God promises that His Word will provide light and guidance for my life.

This is a precious promise that each believer can claim. We have God's assurance that if we study His Word, the Bible, we will receive His guidance and light. Therefore, we will not lose our way. Do you often find that you are wandering without direction in life and don't know which way to turn? Look to God's Word each day and you will discover direction and the light of life.

<u>Lessons and Truths</u>:

1.   God guides through His Word.
2.   God's Word is truth for life.

3.　　God's Word is light to the world. Jesus was the ultimate expression of God's Word.

4.　　God cares about me and the way I live.

Prayer: Lord, plant in my heart a desire to study your Word and meditate on your truths. Direct me and provide light so that I may walk, daily, in a way that is pleasing to you. I know you are faithful and that your Word is true. Thank you for providing the ultimate light in Jesus, your indwelling Holy Spirit, and the Bible to guide me in your ways. Amen

What is my response to God's promise?

How much time do I spend reading, studying, and meditating on God's Word each week? ____

____

____

Do I need to raise my expectations as I do this study? ________

____

____

How can I use God's Word each day to guide my life? ________

____

____

Promise Confirmation: Psalm 119:129-133, Proverbs 30:5, John 1:1-5, 14, John 8:12, Hebrews 4:12

<u>Day 4</u>

Glorious Provision

Philippians 4:19

"*And my God will supply every need of yours according to his riches in glory in Christ Jesus.*"

<u>**Promise:**</u> God promises to supply for my every *need*.

Does God promise in this verse to supply everything I *want*? NO! The key to this promise is the word *need*. There is a great difference between what I *want* and what I truly *need*. Sometimes I think I, desperately, need something, and when I think about it more seriously, I realize that it is only what I want or desire. God has all the riches of the universe at His command, but He gives me only what I *need*. This brings me comfort, as often times I seem to be my own worst enemy, wanting things that will cause me harm. God knows what is best for me, and I am comforted that He will always tend to my needs.

<u>**Lessons and Truths:**</u>

1.　　God has infinite resources available to me through Christ Jesus.

2.   God is sovereign over all circumstances, places, and people.

3.   God in His omniscience knows all my needs.

4.   God can and will provide for me. He loves and cares about me, and I am important to Him.

Prayer: Lord, create in me an attitude of gratitude for your abundant provision and care. Guide me to ask only for those things that I truly *need*. Give me discernment about things that are really only *wants*. Increase my faith so that I can live with greater trust in you and assurance of your provision. Amen.

What is my response to God's promise?

Am I thanking God regularly for His provision and care for me?

____

What do I need to thank Him for today? _______________

____

____

Do I truly trust God to provide for *all* my needs? ___________

____

____

What am I facing today where I need God's provision? ______

____

____

Promise Confirmation: Exodus 16:9-15, 35, Psalm 23:1, Psalm 34:8-10, Matthew 6:25-34

<u>Day 5</u>

The Only Way

John 14:6

"Jesus answered, 'I am the way, and the truth, and the life. No one comes to the Father except through me.'"

<u>Promise</u>: God promises that Jesus is the **only** way to find God, know the truth about God, and possess eternal life.

Jesus himself tells us plainly that He and He alone is the way to find God. He is not a way but *the way*. Many people seek God through nature, other religions, and within themselves, but Jesus very explicitly said that HE is the way to God. Jesus also says HE is the truth of God and that in Him we will find life. Life in Jesus is full, rich, and eternal. Life through Jesus is an eternal adventure!

<u>Lessons and Truths</u>:

1. Jesus is the only way to come into a relationship with God.
2. Through Jesus we have a life that is full and eternal.

3.   Jesus reveals the truth that is God and about God.

Prayer: Lord, thank you for sending Jesus to provide a way for me to be in a right relationship with you through His sacrifice on the cross. Without His death, I would still be lost. You are merciful and provide me with the truth of your Word and promise life eternally with you. Allow me to share your truth with someone today. Amen.

What is my response to God's promise?

How am I using God's truth—His Word—in my life?

____

____

____

____

Do I believe that Jesus is the *only way* to have a relationship with God? ____

____

____

____

If in doubt, review today's Promise Confirmation scriptures for assurance.

Promise Confirmation: John 1:4, 14, 17-18, Acts 4:12, 1 Timothy 2:3-6, Titus 2:11-14, Hebrews 10:19-23

<u>Day 6</u>

Confident Living

Deuteronomy 31: 6

"*Be strong and courageous. Do not be afraid or terrified because of them, for the LORD your God goes with you; he will never leave you nor forsake you.*"

<u>**Promise:**</u> God promises to go *wherever* I go and never leave me.

When the children of Israel received this promise, they were about to enter the land promised by God. They were going to be facing their enemies in battle. This certainty of God's presence is repeated over and over in the Bible. God desires that we have confidence and trust in Him. He does not want us to fear people, circumstances or things, but to live with assurance in Him.

<u>**Lessons and Truths:**</u>

1.   Following God requires me to be courageous and unafraid.
2.   God is omnipresent.

3.   God is faithful and trustworthy at all times and in all circumstances.

4.   God keeps His promises.

<u>Prayer</u>: Lord, lead me to a deeper faith and help me to realize that you are with me at all times and in all circumstances. Give me a sense of your presence today and help me to live more confidently knowing you are always with me. Amen.

<u>What is my response to God's promise?</u>

Am I relying on God's presence to daily encourage and strengthen me? _______________________________________

Where do I need His strength and courage today? ____________

____

____

Do I believe with all my heart that God is *always* with me and God will *never* leave me? _______________________

____

____

How should these truths be affecting my life? _______________

____

____

____

<u>Promise Confirmation</u>:   Psalm 139:7-10, Matthew 28:18-20, Hebrews 13:5-6

<u>Day 7</u>

Eternal Endurance

Isaiah 51:7-8

"Hear me, you who know what is right, you people who have my law in your hearts: Do not fear the reproach of men or be terrified by their insults.

For the moth will eat them up like a garment; the worm will devour them like wool. But my righteousness will last forever, my salvation through all generations."

<u>Promise</u>: God promises believers that His righteousness is eternal and His salvation will endure throughout all generations.

When you play a game, who do you choose to be on your team? Usually, I like to choose the most competent person for the game. Who is most competent when it comes to life and reaching godly goals? God! He is greater than anything I can ever face. He assures me that He will endure eternally and He will save me. I need to believe and not focus on the turmoil that surrounds me. I will keep my focus on Almighty God!

<u>**Lessons and Truths**</u>:

1. God's Word can abide in my heart.
2. God's Word teaches rightness for living.
3. Men are temporal and God is eternal.
4. Men use fear to control others; God is greater than any of their plans.
5. God cares for sinful man and has provided a way for salvation.
6. God's plan of salvation is immutable — the same yesterday, today, and forever, unchanging from generation to generation.

Prayer: Lord, teach me through your Word as I seek to claim your promises. Through me, show your righteousness to others. Give me courage to face the tough situations without fear and depend upon you for strength and victory. I am so thankful that you are unchanging and for the assurance, which your character brings to my life. Amen.

<u>**What is my response to God's promise?**</u>

Where am I experiencing fear and in need of dependence upon God for victory? ___________________________________

____

Where do I need to *put on* Christ's righteousness today? _____

____

____

<u>**Promise Confirmations**</u>: Psalm 119:144, 2 Timothy 1:9-12, Hebrews 13:8

<u>Day 8</u>

A Solid Hope

Hebrews 10:23

"*Let us hold unswervingly to the hope we profess, for he who promised is faithful.*"

<u>Promise:</u> God promises us a solid hope that we may cling to in Christ.

I looked up **swerve** in the dictionary and it means*: to turn aside or cause to turn aside from a straight line.* When I think of this in biblical terms, it means I need to hold onto what I have in Christ and not become sidetracked. What do I have in Christ that is worth holding onto when the world swirls around me? Faith in Christ gives me hope, salvation, eternal life, and the Holy Spirit, who indwells me. He is with me each and every day. He provides me with love, peace, assurance, and guidance through His Word. I can have a personal relationship with Almighty God. What earthly thing can compare to the riches I have in Christ?

<u>**Lessons and Truths**</u>:

1. God is faithful.
2. God gives me hope for my life now and a future through Christ.
3. God desires that I cling to Jesus, my hope, without wavering.
4. Faith enables me to stand firm during the hard times in life.

<u>Prayer</u>: Lord, thank you for sending Jesus to die on the cross for my sins and for bringing me into a right relationship with you. My hope in Christ brings eternal hope and assurance that I will be with you in heaven. I can experience a better quality of life here and now through Him. Cause me to love you more each day and trust, completely, in your great faithfulness. Amen.

<u>**What is my response to God's promise?**</u>

How am I trusting in God's faithfulness each day? __________

____

____

What am I doing to strengthen my faith so I can stand firm?

____

____

<u>Promise Confirmation</u>: Deuteronomy 7:9, Psalm 42:5, Colossians 1:27, 1 Thessalonians 5:8-11, 2 Thessalonians 3:3, 1 Timothy 4:9-10, Hebrews 6:17-20, Hebrews 11:1,6, 1 John 3:1-3

<u>Day 9</u>

Standing on a Firm Foundation

2 Timothy 2:19

"But God's firm foundation stands, bearing this seal: 'The Lord knows those who are his,' and, 'Let everyone who names the name of the Lord depart from iniquity.'"

<u>Promise:</u> God promises a firm foundation for our faith. He knows each one He has chosen.

Have you ever played the game Jenga? You build a tower and then slowly pull out blocks, one by one, until your tower crumbles. My faith is built upon Jesus, who is a firm foundation. Life events, trials, and crises all pull at me to shake or weaken my faith. This verse assures me that God knows my trials and will stand with me. He will not allow me to crumble and fall if I remain rooted in Him. Turning away from sin will strengthen my faith and keep me standing firmly with Jesus.

<u>**Lessons and Truths**</u>:

1. The firm foundation of our faith is Jesus Christ.
2. God's seal is given by the Holy Spirit.
3. The Lord is omniscient and knows those who believe in Him.
4. Knowing Christ demands that I turn from sin and follow Him.

<u>**Prayer:**</u> Lord, thank you for choosing me and knowing me personally. Help me to learn from your Word and be able to stand firm in my faith. Give me opportunities today to share my love for you and boldness to speak your truth. Show me where sin is affecting my witness and help me to eliminate it from my life. Amen.

<u>What is my response to God's promise?</u>

How am I trying to walk with Him and turning away from sin?

____

____

Is Christ the foundation of my faith? ____________________

____

____

Review today's Promise Confirmation verses for assurance your foundation is in Jesus.

<u>**Promise Confirmation**</u>: Isaiah 28:16, Isaiah 49:16, John 10:14-15, John 15:19, 1 Corinthians 3:11, 2 Corinthians 1:21-22, Ephesians 2:19-22, 2 Thessalonians 2:13-14, 1 Peter 3:10-12, 1 John 1:8-10

Day 10

We Are Family

Matthew 12:46-50

"*While Jesus was still talking to the crowd, his mother and brothers, stood outside, wanting to speak to him. Someone told him, 'Your mother and brothers are standing outside, wanting to speak to you.' He replied to him, 'Who is my mother, and who are my brothers?' Pointing to his disciples, he said, 'Here are my mother and my brothers. For whoever does the will of my Father in heaven is my brother and sister and mother.'*"

Promise: God promises that belief in Him, and obedience to Him, brings us into His family.

Have you ever thought about what it means to be in God's family? It is the best of our earthly family and much more! It is security, love, care, trust, and gatherings with family members. The best family reunion ever will be in heaven, as there will be no bickering, mourning, crying or hurt feelings. Our membership in God's family is evidenced by our obedience and love for one another. Praise God for His great mercy and love for us through

Jesus and for giving us a new family through Him. Cherish and love your brothers and sisters in Christ. They are your forever family.

<u>Lessons and Truth</u>:
1. Belief and obedience bring me into God's family.
2. God is relational and desires a relationship with me.
3. God is my Father, and I am brought into His family when I accept Jesus as my Savior.
4. Being in God's family requires treating other believers as family.

<u>Prayer</u>: Lord, thank you for sending Jesus to die for my sins so that I can be in a family relationship with you. I know you want me to glorify you in all that I do. Help me to be the best brother, sister, or mother I can be. Give me greater love and care for my earthly family, as well as those from my spiritual family. Pull me closer to your Word that I may walk in obedience to you. Amen.

<u>What is my response to God's promise?</u>

Have I chosen to be in God's family by believing in Jesus?

____

If you have not done this, do it right now. Confess your sins before God, profess your belief in Jesus as His Son who died for your sins, ask Jesus to be the Lord of your life and to send His Holy Spirit to indwell you. Now you are in God's family—welcome!

What kind of brother, sister, or mother am I in God's family?

____

<u>Promise Confirmation</u>: Mark 3:34-35, Romans 8: 28-30, Hebrews 2:10-12

<u>Day 11</u>

Incorruptible Treasures

Matthew 6:19-21

"*Do not store up for yourselves treasures on earth, where moth and rust destroy, and where thieves break in and steal. But store up for yourselves treasures in heaven, where moth and rust do not destroy, and where thieves do not break in and steal. For where your treasure is, there your heart will be also.*"

<u>**Promise:**</u> God promises incorruptible, heavenly treasures if I will set my heart on eternal, not earthly, things.

Have you ever given thought to what you can take with you when you die? Things that we buy, make, achieve in our jobs, and learn about the world will be of no value in heaven. We won't be able to take them with us. Only those things with eternal value will endure and be with us in heaven. Relationships, kindnesses done for others, faith in Jesus, work for the kingdom, witnessing, preaching, studying about God, memorizing Scripture, prayer, eternal life, righteousness, joy, peace and growing more like Jesus are all things that will be with us eternally. Where are you storing up treasures?

<u>Lessons and Truths</u>:
1.   Godly treasures are eternal and have great value.
2.   Earthy valuables are temporal, just for now.
3.   The things I treasure reveal my heart attitude and motivation in life.
4.   God's rewards are far greater than anything I could possess now.

<u>Prayer</u>: Lord, help me to examine the goals that are motivating me today. Create in me a *heart* attitude that seeks to place your treasures above the desire for things that surround me. Open my eyes to see the treasures you reveal and provide in your Word each day. Amen.

<u>What is my response to God's promise?</u>

What do the things I value in life say about my *heart* attitudes?

____

____

____

Which of God's treasures do I want to see more of in my life?

____

____

<u>Promise Confirmation</u>: Proverbs 23:4-5, Matthew 13:44-46, Luke 12:32-34, 1 Corinthians 3:12-15, 1 Timothy 6:17-19

<u>Day 12</u>

Godly Living

Joshua 1:8

"*This Book of the Law shall not depart from your mouth, but you shall meditate on it day and night, so that you may be careful to do according to all that is written in it. For then you will make your way prosperous and then you will have good success.*"

<u>Promise</u>: God promises that living by His Word each day, and keeping my focus on Him will bring me prosperity and success.

What is prosperity and success in God's eyes? God explains in this promise that following His Word, keeping our thinking on His precepts, and living a God-driven life will glorify Him. Would that kind of life bring you happiness and success in relationships? Will it provide freedom from stress, guilt over sin and worry? God's ways are in contrast to the self-driven and self-gratifying goals of this world. God knows that following the world's standards leads to glorifying self. Which goals do you want motivating you?

<u>**Lessons and Truths:**</u>

1. I am to meditate on God's Word in order to absorb its truths.
2. God's Word demands careful attention.
3. Living God's way brings God-given blessings.

<u>**Prayer:**</u> Lord, thank you for your Word and your promise to bless me if I will live by your Word. Give me a heart to read, meditate, and study your Word faithfully. Help me to set godly goals that will glorify you. Thank you for what you have already done and what you will do in and through me. Amen.

<u>What is my response to God's promise?</u>

What am I doing to put God's Word into my daily life so that I can live by it? _______________________________________

____

____

How has God already blessed me since I began this study?

____

____

____

<u>**Promise Confirmation**</u>: Deuteronomy 6:4-9, Psalm 1:1-3, Psalm 103:20-22, James 1:22-25

Day 13

Growing God's Way

John 15:1-2

"*I am the true vine, and my Father is the gardener. He cuts off every branch in me that bears no fruit, while every branch that does bear fruit he prunes so that it will be even more fruitful.*"

Promise: God promises pruning (discipline, training) to make me grow in Christ so that my life will be more fruitful.

I love my garden and the beautiful flowers and vegetables that I grow. They are pleasing to look at and a joy to eat. The image given in these verses is that just as I need to cultivate, prune, and water my garden, God needs to do the same with me. He directs, guides, and causes me to hurt at times to produce a more steadfast character that is deeply rooted in Jesus. I don't particularly like the pruning, as it is often difficult, but I can look back and see how those hard times caused me to draw nearer to Him and walk more closely in trust. I know that God wants the very best for me and that He is good. His ways are not my ways, yet He will cause me to grow and develop that steadfast character He desires, if I will trust Him and depend fully upon Jesus to guide, mold, and uplift me.

<u>Lessons and Truths</u>:
1. Jesus is the source of growth and life for the believer.
2. A believer's life must show fruit.
3. God disciplines those He loves.
4. God's pruning produces even more fruit in my life.
5. God tends to me. He oversees my growth and productivity.

<u>Prayer</u>: Father God, I know that pruning and discipline are difficult when they come into my life. I want to joyfully thank you for loving me and molding my character so that I will be able to stand firm in my faith. Produce in me your fruit that I can be used more effectively for your kingdom. Let others see Jesus in me. Amen.

<u>What is my response to God's promise?</u>

What kind of fruit is evident in my life? *Galatians 5:22-23a says, "But the fruit of the Spirit is love, joy, peace, patience, kindness, goodness, faithfulness, gentleness and self-control."*

____

____

____

____

<u>Promise Confirmation</u>:   Psalm 25:8-10, Proverbs 3:11-12, Matthew 7:16-20, Romans 8:28, Ephesians 5:8-11, James 1:2-4

Day 14

Godly Commitment

Psalm 37:5-6

"*Commit your way to the LORD; trust in him, and he will act. He will bring forth your righteousness as the light, and your justice as the noonday.*"

Promise: God promises to act on my behalf, bring out righteousness and justice for me if I will commit myself to Him and trust Him.

How are you at commitment? Do you start new things with great enthusiasm just to let them go in a day or a week? Learning to commit to the LORD is a lifetime process that increases as we study His Word, pray, and seek to follow Him. Truly committing to Him, in both faith and action, allows us to walk in God's light and see His righteousness and justice more clearly. Will you persevere in God's pathway, allowing Him to mold and shape you into the righteous person He desires you to be?

<u>**Lessons and Truths**</u>**:**

1. God is good and wants only good things for me.
2. Following God requires trust and commitment.
3. God has the power to mold and shape my character.
4. God is just and righteous.

<u>**Prayer**</u>**:** Lord, create in me a spirit of commitment to you that I may grow and see evidence of righteousness and justice in my life. I know that you are good and that you want only good things for me. Help me to trust you fully so that I can grow and become more like Jesus each day. Amen.

<u>What is my response to God's promise?</u>

Am I fully trusting God and committing myself to following Him? What evidence is there in my life that this is happening?

____

____

____

Where do I see godly righteousness in my life?_____________

____

____

____

<u>**Promise Confirmation**</u>: 1 Samuel 7:3-4, Psalm 103:6, Psalm 145:17-20, Isaiah 30:18, Matthew 7:11, 2 Corinthians 5:20-21, 1 Peter 2:23-25

<u>Day 15</u>

Salvation Assured

Romans 10:9-10

"That if you confess with your mouth, 'Jesus is Lord,' and believe in your heart that God raised him from the dead, you will be saved. For it is with your heart that you believe and are justified, and it is with your mouth that you confess and are saved."

<u>**Promise:**</u> God promises salvation to those who confess Jesus as Lord and believe He died and rose again.

God has a wonderful plan to save us, which requires faith in Jesus and His work on the cross. We do not have to fulfill a list of good works to be saved. In no way can we earn God's favor without faith in His Son. Hebrews 11:6 says, *"And without faith it is impossible to please God, because anyone who comes to him must believe that he exists and that he rewards those who earnestly seek him."* All God requires of us is faith. Many people spend their lives fighting, rationalizing, and trying to deny faith. Many spend their lives trying to earn God's good favor and to be good enough for Him. God tells us simply that *only* faith is required. Simple enough. Do you have it?

Lessons and Truths:

1. God hears me when I speak to him.
2. Faith, believing in Jesus, is essential for salvation.
3. God can save me.
4. I am justified by faith in Jesus, not by anything I do.
5, God knows my heart attitude and whether or not my faith in Jesus is real.

Prayer: Lord, thank you for sending Jesus to die for my sins and for His victory over death. Thank you for the gift of faith and the knowledge that I am saved. Lord give me a heart for the unsaved and, especially, those I already know who do not know Jesus as Lord and Savior. Give me opportunities to speak boldly about salvation. Amen.

What is my response to God's promise?

Do you know for *sure* that you are saved? Have you done the following in faith? _______________________________________

Admitted that you are a sinner and confessed your sins specifically? *(Romans 3:10-12)* _______________________

Believe that Jesus is the Son of God and went to the cross for you? *(John 3:16)*________________________________

Prayed and asked Jesus into your heart to be your Lord and Savior? *(1 John 1:9)* ___________________________

Now: Trust you have received Christ into your life, you are sealed by His Holy Spirit and He lives in you. Read: John 1:12-

13, 1 Corinthians 6:19-20, 2 Corinthians 1:21-22.

Who do you know that needs to hear about Jesus? __________

____

____

Promise Confirmation: John 14:6, John 11:25-26, Acts 4:12, Romans 6:23, Titus 3:4-7

<u>Day 16</u>

God, Our Promise Keeper

Jeremiah 32:40-41

"*I will make them an everlasting covenant, that I will not turn away from doing good to them. And I will put the fear of me in their hearts, that they may not turn from me. I will rejoice in doing them good, and I will plant them in this land in faithfulness, with all my heart and all my soul.*"

<u>Promise</u>: God promises He always intends good toward me and He will put a reverence in my heart to keep me connected to Him.

We live in an era where people do not seem to value keeping their word. We also know that if we try to keep our word, and do as we say, it is not always humanly possible. Here, God says that He *does* and *will* keep His promises to us. He is eternally faithful and takes joy in doing good for us. It is a great comfort to know that nothing is impossible for God. He will always keep his promises and He delights in doing good on our behalf!

<u>**Lessons and Truths**</u>:

1. God is eternal and His Word is everlasting.
2. God intends good for me.
3. Reverence (fear) of God helps to keep me connected and focused on Him.
4. God takes joy in doing good towards me.
5. God is faithful.

<u>**Prayer**</u>: Lord, I am so grateful that you keep your promises. I do not need to doubt my salvation, the work of the Holy Spirit within me, my citizenship in heaven, Jesus' intercession on my behalf, or your joy over me being your child. Thank you for the reverence I have toward you and for keeping me connected to you through the work of the Holy Spirit. May I keep walking in your ways and growing in trust and knowledge of you each day. Amen.

<u>What is my response to God's promise?</u>

Knowing God intends only good for me, what do I need to trust Him for today? _______________________________________

____

How can I show reverence and humility towards God?

____

____

____

<u>**Promise Confirmation**</u>: Psalm 103:17-19, Proverbs 19:23, Jeremiah 29:11, Romans 8:28, 2 Corinthians 1:20-22

<u>Day 17</u>

Obtainable Mercy

Proverbs 28:13

"*Whoever conceals his transgressions will not prosper, but he who confesses and forsakes them will obtain mercy.*"

<u>Promise</u>: God promises that confession and turning away from sin will bring mercy, while hiding my sin will bring consequences.

Why does concealing sin cause us to not prosper? Hiding any wrong doing creates guilt, paranoid, fear, and distrust. God knows that hiding wrong doings will lead us further away from Him. To be in a right relationship with God, we need to keep short accounts of our sins and confess daily those things we feel we have done against God and others. True confession and turning away from our sins leads to forgiveness, and it opens us up to receive God's mercy. God is compassionate and kind and will treat us mercifully.

Lessons and Truths:

1. God is forgiving.
2. God is merciful.
3. God is sovereign and can grant me forgiveness and mercy.
4. Hiding or keeping hold of sin will prevent me from being successful and leading the life God intends for me.

Prayer: Lord, cause me to be open with you and regularly confess my sins. Show me where I fall short and need to repent. Help me to turn away from my sin and walk in your ways, that I may obtain your mercy. Thank you that your mercies are new every morning and that you are a loving and forgiving heavenly Father. Amen.

What is my response to God's promise?

Do I confess my sins regularly? What sins do I need to confess to Him today? _______________________________________

____

____

Am I truthful with God about my sin or am I trying to hide something that I am ashamed of? _____________________

____

____

Tell him now and let it go. Receive His mercy.

Promise Confirmation: Psalm 32:1-2, 5, Micah 7:18-20, Romans 6:23, Romans 10:9-13, Ephesians 2:4-10, 1 John 1:8-10

<u>Day 18</u>

Salvation by Faith

Acts 16:30-31

"Then he (the Philippian jailer) brought them (Paul and Silas) out and said, 'Sirs, what must I do to be saved?' And they said, 'Believe in the Lord Jesus, and you will be saved, you and your household.'"

<u>Promise</u>: God promises that faith in Jesus *alone* will bring salvation.

I find this verse extremely comforting, as it clearly states that faith in Jesus is all that we need to attain salvation. We can't buy salvation, nor can we earn salvation. It is a free gift from God through Jesus, when we believe. When we accept the gift of salvation, the Holy Spirit comes to live inside us. Then we desire to do good works and strive to honor Jesus in our lives. Hold firmly to your belief in Jesus and His saving work (His death and resurrection), and you will have the power of the living God at work in your own life. Praise God!

<u>Lessons and Truths</u>:

1.　　Salvation comes through faith in Jesus.

2.   Our salvation affects those that live with us.

3.   Salvation requires me to step forward in faith and accept Jesus and His atoning work on the cross.

~ 56 ~

<u>Prayer</u>: Lord, thank you that I do not have to try to be "good enough" to earn my salvation. Faith in Jesus is all that you require to be able to live for you now and throughout eternity. Help me to accept Jesus and His work on the cross. Use the power of the Holy Spirit within me to live for you each day. Amen.

<u>What is my response to God's promise?</u>

How is my faith growing and drawing me closer to Jesus?

____

____

____

How do those that live with me see Jesus in my life? _________

____

____

____

<u>Promise Confirmation</u>:   John 3:16, John 14:6, Acts 4:12, Romans 10:9-11, Ephesians 2:8-10, Titus 3: 4-7

<u>Day 19</u>

Always Complete

Philippians 1:6

"*And I am sure of this, that he who began a good work in you will bring it to completion at the day of Jesus Christ.*"

<u>**Promise**</u>: God promises that He began a good work in me when I accepted Jesus as my Savior. His faithfulness to me will continue until Christ returns for me.

I love this promise, as it gives me assurance that God will continue to work in my life and will, assuredly, accomplish good through me, until Jesus comes again or I meet Him in heaven. The promises we make on earth are temporal and dependent on our attempts to see things done. God does not work that way. He is eternal and will always accomplish that which He has set out to do. It gives me confidence that my salvation is thought of by God as a good work. He loves and cares for me and wants only good things for me. His work is always completed just as He wants it to be. Praise God!

<u>**Lessons and Truths**</u>:

1.   God never starts something and leaves it incomplete.
2.   God is faithful.
3.   Christ Jesus will return.
4.   God's work is good in me and for me.

<u>**Prayer**</u>: Lord, I am so thankful that you saved me and began a good work in me. I know that being with you is eternal. You will faithfully bring the good work you started in me to a blessed completion. Help me to be responsive, be open to your leading and look to you for strength and encouragement. Give me a voice to speak-out for you and tell others of your good work through Christ. Amen.

<u>What is my response to God's promise</u>?

Am I open to God's leading in my life or do I try to ignore the nudging of the Holy Spirit? ______________________________

____

Do I doubt God's faithfulness? ______________________________

If so, I claim Luke 1:37 and Lamentations 3:22-23.

How have I seen God's faithfulness in my life? ______________

____

____

____

<u>**Promise Confirmation**</u>: Proverbs 16:3-4, Acts 1:9-11, Romans 8:28, Ephesians 2:19-22, 1 Thessalonians 4:16-18

Day 20

It Belongs to God, Thank Goodness!

Deuteronomy 32:43

"*Rejoice with him, O heavens; bow down to him, all gods, for he avenges the blood of his children and takes vengeance on his adversaries. He repays those who hate him and cleanses his people's land.*"

Hebrews 10:30-31

"*For we know him who said, 'Vengeance is mine; I will repay.' And again, 'The Lord will judge his people.' It is a fearful thing to fall into the hands of the living God.*"

<u>**Promise**</u>: God promises vengeance toward those who would seek to take advantage of or kill His children. He considers them His enemies and will judge them as such.

It is a natural tendency to want to get revenge for a wrong done to us. God tells us in His Word that we are to leave revenge, vengeance, judgment, and vindication to Him. Why do you think He wants us to leave that to Him? My thought is that we can become so consumed with getting even, we stop pursuing the things God intends for us to do. Constant focus on revenge opens the door to the sins of hate, discontent, anger, and fear. James 1: 20 tells us that *"the anger of man does not produce the righteousness of God."* Are you willing to let God handle those who have done you wrong? If you are seeking godly peace, you need to be open and willing to do things His way.

<u>Lessons and Truths</u>:
1. God is a vengeful God.
2. God will avenge martyred believers.
3. God will take vengeance on His enemies.
4. God is alive and I should be awed by His omnipotent power.
5. God will judge sin and unbelief and will right the wrongs done to believers.

<u>Prayer</u>: Lord, you are pure and holy and you cannot tolerate evil. You will avenge those who do me wrong. I need to trust you to take care of injustices I may experience. Help me stay focused on you and not be consumed by fear, hate, discontent or anger. I confess _______ as sin and ask you to cleanse me. Fill me with peace today. Amen.

<u>What is my response to God's promise</u>?

Where am I experiencing injustice for the cause of Christ?

____

When have I been awed by God and His power?

____

<u>Promise Confirmation</u>: Psalm 94:1-2 and 22-23, Nahum 1:2-3, Romans 12:19-21

Day 21

God Cares

Nahum 1:7

"*The LORD is good, a refuge in times of trouble. He cares for those who trust in him.*"

Promise: God promises to care for those who believe and trust in Him.

What does it mean to you that God is your refuge? For me, it means that God is the one to whom I can go, He will always love me and have a place for me both physically and spiritually. In Him, I know I will find understanding, comfort, strength, and renewal. What better refuge could I ever have? God's care is available to me because I trust Him and know that He wants only good things for me. His promised care is a great comfort to me.

Lessons and Truths:

1. God is good.

2.   God Himself is a refuge for me, a place of calm, protection, and love. He is   available whenever I need Him.

3.   God cares for believers and desires to shelter them.

Prayer: Lord, thank you that you are there for me when I am struggling. Knowing that you will always be there gives me great comfort and assurance. I know you love and care for me. Show me your heavenly care in the midst of my busy day and lighten my load with your continual presence. Amen.

What is my response to God's promise?

What evidence have I seen in my life that shows God is good and wants the best for me? ________________________________

____

____

Where do I need to seek God's refuge and comfort today?

____

____

____

Promise Confirmation: Psalm 34:8-10, Psalm 46:1-3, Psalm 62:5-8, Proverbs 3:5-6, Lamentations 3:25-26, Matthew 6:25-34, Romans 8:31-32, Philippians 4:4-7 and 4:11-13, 1 Peter 5:6-7

<u>Day 22</u>

Good Plans

Jeremiah 29:11

"'*For I know the plans I have for you,' declares the LORD, 'plans to prosper you and not to harm you, plans to give you hope and a future.'*"

<u>Promise</u>: God promises His plans for my life are good and filled with hope.

This is one of my favorite verses because it plainly states God's intent toward me, and it is *all* good. It means that God loves me and has a plan for my life. I am valued by Him and have a purpose. Once I really got a hold of this concept, my sagging self-esteem was restored. No matter what others think, God is the only one who matters. He loves me and wants good things for me. Following His way will lead me to the good plans He has for me. Give your own self-esteem a boost and memorize this verse, meditate on it, keep it in your heart, and see what a difference it will make!

<u>**Lessons and Truths**</u>:

1. God is sovereign and controls the past, present, and future.
2. God's plans for me are good.
3. God gives hope.
4. Prosperity, safety, and hope come from God.

<u>**Prayer**</u>: Lord, you are sovereign and control the events in my life. Guide me toward a greater trust so I can praise and thank you in all things. Give me hope and confidence in the future. Wrap me in your love. Guard and protect my self-esteem so that I can blossom in you and serve you with a thankful heart. Amen.

<u>What is my response to God's promise?</u>

Where have I experienced God's good plans in the past? _____

____

____

Where am I anxious about the future? ______________________

____

____

____

<u>**Promise Confirmation**</u>: Psalm 33:10-12, Psalm 40:4-5, Isaiah 46:8-11, Lamentations 3:25-26, Matthew 7:11, 1 Timothy 4:9-10

<u>Day 23</u>

A Forgiving Heart

Matthew 6:14-15

"For if you forgive others their trespasses, your heavenly Father will also forgive you, but if you do not forgive others their trespasses, neither will your Father forgive your trespasses."

<u>**Promise:**</u> God promises to forgive the things I do wrong, but I must forgive those who have wronged me in order to receive full restoration in my relationship with Him.

This promised restoration from God requires that I do not harbor grudges, ill feelings, hatred or malice toward those who have wronged me. Why do you suppose God requires this of us? God is our Creator and He knows all things about the events in our lives. He knows how feelings about mistreatment can fester and grow in our minds. It blocks our communication with Him. James 1:14-15 says, *"But each person is tempted when he is lured and enticed by his own desire. Then desire when it has conceived gives birth to sin and sin when it is fully grown brings*

~ 65 ~

forth death." God wants us to be free from sin and knows these feelings need to be given to Him and cleansed from our minds. If we don't, the sin will eat at us and block our relationship with God.

<u>Lessons and Truths</u>:
1. Being forgiven requires having a forgiving heart.
2. God desires that we do not harbor grudges, wrong attitudes, hatred, and resentment as they block a forgiving heart.
3. God's forgiveness is unconditional (no matter what we've done) and my forgiveness of others should be like His.
4. Forgiveness frees you from sin's hold.
5. God knows I desire to be forgiven and that I need to give forgiveness to be whole.

<u>Prayer</u>: Lord, I know you have forgiven my sins and buried them in the deepest sea, never to be seen or heard from again. Through your Holy Spirit, reveal to me where I am acting with an unforgiving heart attitude. Lead me to forgive those who have wronged me. Teach me to be forgiving toward others, just as you have forgiven me. Amen.

<u>What is my response to God's promise?</u>

What is God revealing to me about grudges, resentments, hatred, hurts, wrongs or even my perceived wrongs? _______________

____

Where do I need to seek God's forgiveness for my unforgiving attitude toward others? _______________________________

<u>Promise Confirmation</u>: Matthew 6:9-13, Luke 6:37-38, Colossians 3:12-13, James 2:12-13

A New Nature

2 Corinthians 5:17

"Therefore, if anyone is in Christ, he is a new creation; the old has gone, the new has come."

<u>Promise</u>: God promises that belief in Christ changes you into a new person, with a new nature, and your old sinful nature is gone.

The hope of this verse is that in Christ I can be a new person with new desires, motivation, actions and attitudes. Being in Christ awakens my spirit and aligns me with God and His desires for my life. Is this easy to accomplish? No, for while we are still here on earth, we continue to have fleshly bodies, keeping us anchored to the world. We struggle with putting worldly desires aside and focusing on Christ and what He has for us. It is a glorious struggle that requires us to abide in Christ and walk closely with Him. I strive to discover new things about myself in Christ each day. What an adventure!

<u>Lessons and Truths</u>:

1.	Belief in Christ is life changing.
2.	Once God changes you, it is permanent.
3.	God is consistent and sovereign over all.

<u>Prayer</u>: Lord, create in me a clean heart that I might reflect your glory and show Jesus more and more in my life. Replace my selfish desires and motives with new attitudes and actions based on your Word. Give me self-control so that I can focus on you and lead a life that is pleasing to you. Amen.

<u>What is my response to God's promise?</u>

What changes do I see in myself that are a result of my faith in Christ? ____

____

____

____

What areas in my life do I still need Christ to transform so that I can become more like Him? _______________________________

____

____

____

<u>Promise Confirmation</u>: Isaiah 62:1-3, Galatians 2:20, Colossians 3:5-10, 1 Peter 1:3-4

<u>Day 25</u>

Desires of the Heart

Psalm 37:3-4

"*Trust in the LORD, and do good; dwell in the land and befriend faithfulness. Delight yourself in the LORD, and he will give you the desires of your heart.*"

<u>Promise</u>: God promises to give me the desires of my heart, if I trust and delight in Him, do good and embrace faithfulness.

I have often prayed this verse for friends who struggle with lifelong desires that do not seem to be in God's will for their lives. Young men or women waiting for a godly mate (as they so want to be married), those who desire to have a child and cannot seem to conceive, others waiting on a much needed job, while still others struggle with the job they have, wanting to change directions, etc., these are just some of the things they wrestle with that may be the desires of their hearts. What I pray for those waiting on God's timing and plan is that they will grow in trust and faithfulness. Also, that God would be their delight as they wait upon Him, and that they would be able to focus on

Him for strength and perseverance. Difficult times require me to delight myself in Him and cling to His faithfulness, trusting He has a perfect plan for my life.

<u>Lessons and Truths</u>:
1. God desires a relationship with me.
2. God rewards those who follow Him in faith.
3. Living for God requires faith, trust, and doing good.
4. God knows me and the desires of my heart.

<u>Prayer</u>:   Lord, teach me to trust in you fully, delight myself in your presence, diligently study your Word, and accomplish good things for you. You are omniscient and know before I even ask what my heart desires. I know you have good things planned for my life, so help me to align myself with your will. Increase my faith so that I can see you as totally trustworthy and rely on you as the guide for my life. Amen.

<u>What is my response to God's promise?</u>

What heart desire do I want to share with God today? _______

____

____

Where do I need to improve my walk of faith? ____________

____

____

<u>Promise Confirmation</u>: Psalm 20:4-5, Jeremiah 29:11, Hebrews 10:23, 1 Peter 4:19

<u>Day 26</u>

Treasured Guidance

Psalm 119:11

"*I have hidden your word in my heart that I might not sin against you.*"

<u>Promise</u>: God promises His Word, within me, will help keep me from sinning.

Why do we memorize things (e.g. times tables, mathematical measurements, directions to and from frequented places, names, recipes, songs, etc.)? Memorizing important things keeps them at our fingertips. We can access them whenever we want. We don't need to spend time figuring out how much 6 x 8 equals, we already know. The same principle applies to memorizing Bible verses. When we have God's truth with us at all times, we can recall it quickly and apply it to whatever situation comes up. The Holy Spirit will call to our remembrance verses to help keep us from sinning or to direct our choices. What a wonderful deterrent to sin and idle wandering God has given us. Are you being open to this godly input? Have you memorized verses to keep in your mind to help you in times of need? Why not start today with Psalm 119:11?

<u>Lessons and Truths</u>:
1.   God's Word has the power to deter sin.
2.   God wants his Word in my heart and mind.

<u>Prayer:</u> Lord, thank you for the power your Word has in my life, keeping me focused and directed by you. Oh, Holy Spirit call to my remembrance Biblical truths to help me throughout the day so that my actions are pleasing to you. Give me a desire to memorize your Word so that I may hide it in my heart at all times. Amen.

<u>What is my response to God's promise?</u>

How am I trying to hide God's Word in my heart? __________

____

____

____

How much time am I taking to read and study God's Word each day?____

____

____

<u>Promise Confirmation</u>: Psalm 119:9, Luke 6:46-49, Hebrews 4:12, James 1:22-25

<u>Day 27</u>

The Sufficiency of Grace

2 Corinthians 12:9-10

"But he said to me, 'My grace is sufficient for you, for my power is made perfect in weakness.' Therefore I will boast all the more gladly of my weaknesses, so that the power of Christ may rest upon me. For the sake of Christ, then, I am content with weaknesses, insult, hardship, persecutions, and calamities. For when I am weak, then I am strong."

<u>Promise</u>: God promises that His grace is sufficient, and He can use me despite my imperfections and weaknesses.

I love the word *sufficient* as it means: enough, competent, satisfactory, valid, plenty, plentiful and ample. God wants us to know that no matter what the circumstances, people, or events we face, He alone is enough to meet our needs in the situation. What is God using to meet all of our situations? The promise tells us He is using His grace. Grace is God's unmerited favor, available to us through Jesus' work on the cross. God's grace shows us His character, wisdom, mercy, compassion, love, protection, etc. How fortunate are we that God loves us enough to be the *all in all* for our needs?

<u>Lessons and Truths</u>:
1. God's grace will sustain me in all circumstances.
2. God uses His weak creation (me) to show His glory.
3. God's ways are perfect and powerful.
4. God is sovereign and omniscient over His creation.

<u>Prayer</u>: Lord, thank you that your grace is more than enough to meet any challenge I face. Help me to completely trust and depend on your sufficiency. Use me for your work, as I glorify you in spite of my weaknesses. Amen.

<u>What is my response to God's promise?</u>

Where do I need to depend upon God's sufficiency in my life?

____

____

____

Where do I see God's grace in my life? ___________________

____

____

____

<u>Promise Confirmation</u>: Psalm 84:11-12, Psalm 145:8-9, 1 Corinthians 1:25, Ephesians 2:4-10, Hebrews 4:16, 1 Peter 5: 10-11

<u>Day 28</u>

Suiting Up for Battle

Ephesians 6:13

"Therefore put on the full armor of God, so that when the day of evil comes, you may be able to stand your ground, and after you have done everything, to stand."

<u>Promise</u>: God promises His armor will enable me to stand firmly against Satan's attacks. God's armor is truth, righteousness, the gospel of peace, faith, salvation, the sword of the spirit (God's Word) and prayer. This godly armor is described piece by piece in Ephesians 6:14-18.

God tells us to be prepared for Satan's attacks and put on His armor. How many of us take this seriously in our daily lives? Do we recognize the lies that Satan sends out through our culture regarding marriage? What about the lies that we need bigger and better things, power and prestige, or independence to pursue our own destiny? Where is God in our day to day interactions with people? Are we kind, loving, and willing to go the extra mile to help someone? We need to take God at His

Word and confront the assaults from our culture with His armor, so that we can guard our hearts, show love and service to others. Let us put on God's armor for successful living each day.

<u>Lessons and Truths</u>:

1. God's armor protects me in both physical and spiritual battles.
2. God's armor fully covers me.
3. God desires me to stand firm in my faith.
4. Our world contains evil that desires to defeat and destroy our faith.
5. God wants me to do my best and then remain standing in Him.
6. God is more powerful than Satan.

<u>Prayer</u>: Lord, you have given me an armor to be able to fight against Satan's attacks. Help me clothe myself with your armor daily, through your Word and prayer. Give me determination and resolve to stand for you. Bind Satan from undermining my confidence and make me bold for you. Amen.

<u>What is my response to God's promise?</u>

How am I arming myself to battle for God each day? _________

____

Where do I need to stand more firmly for God?______________

____

____

<u>Promise Confirmation</u>: Joshua 1:7-9, Romans 13:11-12, 2 Corinthians 6:3-10, Ephesians 6:10-18, James 1:2

<u>Day 29</u>

The Eyes of God

2 Chronicles 16:8b-9a

"Yet when you relied on the LORD, he delivered them into your hand. For the eyes of the LORD range throughout the earth to strengthen those whose hearts are fully committed to him."

<u>Promise</u>: God promises to search the whole earth for committed believers and to strengthen and deliver them through His omniscient power.

I have always loved this verse. It gives me a great mental picture of the eyes of God looking down upon me. He is not just looking, lazily but actively searching to protect and keep me from harm. To receive God's strength to the fullest, I need to walk with Him daily and be committed to Him. What that looks like in each life will be different. I know to stay committed to Him, I need to keep my focus on Him through daily Bible study, prayer, and fellowship with believers. What does your life of commitment look like? God wants to give us His strength and empower us to do His work in this world. Let's get our hearts and minds committed to serve Him today!

Lessons and Truths:

1. I can rely upon God.
2. He can and will deliver me.
3. God is constantly looking out for me; He is omnipresent and sovereign.
4. God desires my heart be fully committed to Him.

Prayer: Lord, I know you love me and are with me at all times. Be my shield, rock, and protector, as you strengthen me to do your work. Keep me walking close to you, that I may draw upon your strength and stay fully committed to you. Show me, through your Word and other believers, what it means to be fully committed. Lead me in your ways. Amen.

What is my response to God's promise?

What is hindering me from fully committing to Jesus?

____

____

____

Where do I need to increase or improve my commitment to Him?

____

____

____

Promise Confirmation: Psalm 139:1-10, Ezekiel 34:11-12, John 10: 27-30

Day 30

Chosen to Belong

1 Samuel 12:22

"For the LORD will not forsake his people, for his great name's sake, because it has pleased the LORD to make you a people for himself."

Promise: God promises He has chosen me to be His own. He will not leave me or give me up. I am eternally His.

Even though this promise was first spoken to the nation of Israel, it is just as true today for us believers. Each of us has been chosen by God and we all belong to Him. The phrase "for his great name's sake" speaks about God's love, mercy, and grace to us. It is that divine grace, or unmerited favor, of God's choosing, which gives this promise His assurance. He will not leave us because He is faithful and does not change His mind. James 1:17 says, *"Every good gift and every perfect gift is from above, coming down from the Father of lights with whom there is no variation or shadow due to change."* Once God has chosen us, we know with assurance that He will not change His mind about us belonging to Him. Praise God!

<u>Lessons and Truths</u>:
1. God chose me for eternity. Once I accept Jesus as my Savior, I am sealed by the Holy Spirit for eternity as belonging to Him.
2. God treats me with His grace, or unmerited favor, because He is merciful.
3. By His grace, I am saved!

<u>Prayer</u>: Lord, I am so undeserving of your love and mercy. Thank you for sending Jesus to die for my sins so that I can remain with you forever. You are unchanging and once I accepted Jesus as my savior, I belonged to you for eternity. Help me to live today as your chosen, to walk in the assurance of your love and mercy. Help me to be a witness for you in all I say or do. Amen.

<u>What is my response to God's promise?</u>

How have I seen God's mercy and grace in my life? _________

____

____

____

What can I do today to show I was chosen by God? _________

____

____

____

<u>Promise Confirmation</u>: Psalm 33:11-12, John 15:19, Ephesians 1:3-10, 1:13-14 and 2:8-10, 2 Thessalonians 2:13-14

Day 31

Empowered Living

2 Timothy 1:7

"*For God did not give us a spirit of timidity, but a spirit of power, of love and of self-discipline.*"

Promise: God promises power, love, and self-discipline through His Holy Spirit.

God does not want us to have a spirit of timidity. Being timid in spirit means living with a sense of fear, lacking in self-confidence, or being shy. God wants us boldly walking and trusting Him, as we encounter various trials each day. Through the Holy Spirit, He empowers us, and covers us with His love. He assures us that though Him, we can conquer our negative actions, bad habits, and sinful desires, which would lead us to turn away from Him. Paul said it most eloquently in Romans 8:37, *"No, in all these things we are more than conquerors through him who loved us."* Let us live each day with a spirit of confidence and boldness!

<u>Lessons and Truths</u>:

1. God gives confidence to believers.
2. God can create in me a character that surpasses anything I have within myself.
3. God is Almighty and Sovereign.

<u>Prayer</u>: Lord, you are the Almighty One who can mold and shape me into a beautiful creation for your glory. You, and you alone, have the power to transform me. Give me a bold spirit that will allow me to witness and live each day without fear. With your spirit within me, I am confident that my old habits will die away and that I can, indeed, be a conqueror through Christ. Amen.

<u>What is your response to God's promise?</u>

Where am I experiencing fear and need to ask God to replace it with confidence? _______________________________________

____

____

What habits or desires do I need God to change in me?_______

____

____

____

<u>Promise Confirmation</u>:   Proverbs 28:1, Acts 4:31, Romans 8:37, 2 Corinthians 3:4-6, Titus 2:11-14

Day 32

Glorious Flight

1 Thessalonians 4:16-18

"*For the Lord himself will descend from heaven with a cry of command, with the voice of an archangel, and with the sound of a trumpet of God. And the dead in Christ will rise first. Then we who are alive, who are left, will be caught up together with them in the clouds to meet the Lord in the air, and so we will always be with the Lord. Therefore encourage one another with these words.*"

Promise: The Lord promises to return to earth with a command and fanfare, calling those dead in Christ and the still living believers to meet Him in the air. After His return, we will be with Him forever.

There are a lot of different opinions about the *end- time events*, however, this scene is very vivid and clear. Jesus will return, as He said He would, and it will be a glorious, noisy, and happy event. After His return, we are promised we will be with Him forever. I love to visualize this event and look forward to the extreme joy I will feel. The timing is known only to God, but we do know for sure that it *will* happen just as He has said. What a glorious day that will be!

<u>Lessons and Truths</u>:
1. Jesus will return as He promised.
2. When Jesus returns, all believers, past and present, will be there.
3. Jesus' return begins our time with Him forever.
4. God wants us to be encouraged and to look forward to Christ's return.

<u>Prayer</u>: Lord, you alone know the time and place of the end-time events. Only you know when all your work will be accomplished. Cause me to fully trust you and tirelessly work for your kingdom until the time comes. Give me a sense of urgency to boldly speak to others about Christ, so they may come into your kingdom, too. Amen.

<u>What is my response to God's promise?</u>

What difference does it make in my life to know that Christ will return one day? _______________________________________

____

If today were the day, who do I know that would be left behind?

____

Pray for their salvation and talk to them about Jesus.

<u>Promise Confirmation</u>: John 14:3, Acts 1:10-11, Colossians 3:1-4, Revelation 21:1-4

<u>Day 33</u>

Purposeful Waiting

Psalm 31:23-24

"*Love the LORD, all you his saints! The LORD preserves the faithful but abundantly repays the one who acts in pride. Be strong, and let your heart take courage, all you who wait for the LORD!*"

Promise: God promises to preserve those who faithfully follow Him and allows those who refuse to follow His ways to reap the consequences for their actions.

We all know that all actions bring consequences, from the small child that touches the hot stove to the adult who speeds while driving. We know that poor choices lead to unpleasant consequences. Good choices like studying for a test, paying taxes or dealing honestly with others, brings positive results. This promise assures us that God will preserve those who endeavor to follow His ways, even if we don't see those results right away. He admonished us to be strong and courageous, as we wait for His perfect timing. We need to walk by faith and trust Him for the results.

<u>**Lessons and Truths**</u>:

1. God is worthy of my love and praise.
2. Waiting on God's timing requires courage and strength.
3. Acting prideful leads to God-ordained consequences.
4. God rewards those who follow Him in faith.

<u>Prayer</u>: Lord, you are sovereign and in control of all things. Give me patience to wait for your ways and not follow my own desires. Open my eyes that I may discern those things that will result in negative consequence because of poor choices, based on my own desires. Fortify me with courage and strength that I may wait upon you and follow you each day. Amen.

<u>What is my response to God's promise?</u>

Where do I see prideful ways that have crept into my daily life?

____

____

____

Where does God have me waiting right now that requires patience? _______________________________

____

____

<u>Promise Confirmation</u>: Psalm 27:13-14, Psalm 97:10, Psalm 145:20, Proverbs 16:18, Isaiah 40:30-31, Hebrews 10:35-36

<u>Day 34</u>

A Straight Path

Proverbs 3:5-6

"*Trust in the LORD with all your heart, and do not lean on your own understanding. In all your ways acknowledge him, and he will make straight your paths.*"

<u>**Promise:**</u> God promises to make my path in life straight, if I will trust and acknowledge Him.

Being prideful can get us into a lot of trouble. Thinking *we* know what's best for us and that we can make decisions without God's input is what this promise addresses. God knows if we make our own decisions, we will turn away from Him. We will, eventually, move toward self-gratification and self-promotion. God wants us to trust Him, live by His Word, and use His wisdom. Seeking God's advice and direction reveals how much we trust Him. We know He will lead us in the right direction.

<u>**Lessons and Truths**</u>:

1.   God is trustworthy.
2.   God's wisdom and understanding far exceeds my own.
3.   God desires that I show my dependence upon Him with a heart attitude of trust.
4.   God's way is the direct path in life and leads to fruitfulness and purpose.

<u>Prayer</u>: Lord, I am guilty of thinking that I know what's best for my life, and that I can make my own decisions without your help. Guide me to a greater trust and understanding of your ways. Increase my faith and show me your way through your Word. Guide me through the power of the Holy Spirit. Let the peace in my heart confirm that I am doing what you desire and going where you are leading me. Amen.

<u>What is my response to God's promise?</u>

Where am I showing that I trust and depend on God in my life?

____

____

Where am I trying to live by my own wisdom? _______________

____

____

Pray about this and give it to God today.

<u>Promise Confirmation</u>: Job 12:13, Psalm 16:11, Proverbs 4:10-13, John 8:12, Ephesians 1:7-9, 1 John 1:5-7

Day 35

Water of Life

John 4:13-14

"*Jesus answered, 'Everyone who drinks this water will be thirsty again, but whoever drinks the water I give him will never thirst. Indeed, the water I give him will become in him a spring of water welling up to eternal life.'*"

Promise: God promises that belief in Jesus Christ gives eternal life.

We can all think of different kinds of water: polluted, filtered, spring, murky, silt-filled, ice cold, warm, mineral and now flavored. Water is the liquid of life, and we would survive only a few days without it. Jesus is the *only* One who could ever offer water that gives eternal life. Faith in Jesus is the key to receiving this kind of life-giving water. It doesn't cost money, yet it is priceless, and to receive it, you only have to believe. Is your cup full of His living water?

Lessons and Truths:

1.   God gives me hope of an eternal life with Him.

2.   God's life becomes a well-spring within, nurturing and saving me.

3.   The water of life that God gives quenches my soul.

4.   Faith in Jesus leads to eternal life.

Prayer: Father, open my eyes that I may see the many blessings that come from receiving Jesus as my Savior. Let my faith in Jesus cause me to be full and overflowing, as I seek to share my faith with others. Nurture me with your Spirit and lead me to complete trust in you today. Amen.

What is my response to God's promise?

Do I know for sure that I have eternal life? Look up John 3:16, 14:6 and Acts 4:12 for assurance. _____________________

____

____

How am I allowing God to feed me with His living water?

____

____

____

Promise Confirmation: John 5:24, John 6:40, Romans 6:23, 1 Timothy 1:16, 1 John 5:11-13, 20

<u>Day 36</u>

Living Sacrificially

Romans 12:1-2

"*I appeal to you therefore, brothers, by the mercies of God, to present your bodies as a living sacrifice, holy and acceptable to God, which is your spiritual worship. Do not be conformed to this world, but be transformed by the renewal of your mind, that by testing you may discern what is the will of God, what is good and acceptable and perfect.*"

<u>Promise</u>: God promises transformation, renewal of my mind and life, if I live sacrificially for Him, seeking His will and not worldly fulfillments.

How hard is it to get your mind off worldly things? Sometimes, it seems impossible to stop thinking about my wants and desires, they can fill my waking thoughts. Prayer, reading God's Word, listening to Christian music, or talking with a Christian friend about my thoughts are some of the ways I let God transform me so I can remain aligned with His will for my life. Is it easy? No, but the benefits of God's love and care, salvation and hope are countless beyond measure. Will you let God transform you today so that your actions and words glorify Him? Are you open to God's leading and mercy today?

Lessons and Truths:
1. God is merciful.
2. God desires for me to live a holy life.
3. God's standards are not the same as the world's standards.
4. God can and does transform and renew me.
5. God's will is perfect, good, and the very best for me.

Prayer: Lord, thank you for your mercy and strength. Learning to live for you in this world is hard. I struggle with worldly desires that attempt to take first place in my life. Help me to focus on you and seek your guidance. Show me your perfect will, as I pray and study your Word so that I may better live for you. Amen.

What is my response to God's promise?

Where am I struggling with God's will? ____________________

____

____

Does my life reflect God's standards for holiness or the world's? Where do I need to make some changes to better reflect God in my life? ____

____

Promise Confirmation: Psalm 40:1-4 and 8, Jeremiah 29:11, 2 Corinthians 3:16-18, 1 John 2:15-17

<u>Day 37</u>

Resting in the Lord

1 Kings 8:56

"*Praise be to the LORD, who has given rest to his people Israel just as he promised. Not one word has failed of all the good promises he gave through his servant Moses.*"

<u>Promise</u>: God promises faithfulness and rest in Him.

Can you imagine being able to keep every promise you ever made? For us, it is totally impossible, but God assures us through His Word, which testifies to His promise-keeping ability. He wants us to rest in the fact that He will do as He promises. We needn't have the slightest doubt. We can rest in His ability to care for us and keep us. He did this for the children of Israel and He can do the same for us! Be encouraged today, rely upon God to keep you. He has faithfully promised.

<u>Lessons and Truths</u>:

1.   God is faithful; He keeps His promises.
2.   Believers can find rest in the LORD.

3.   God is sovereign and will see that all is fulfilled, just as He has promised.

Prayer: Lord, the world is in such turmoil and the problems seem so great. Help me to rest in you and trust you for solutions, now and in the future. Build my faith and help me to see evidence of your fulfilled promises in my life. Give me rest in you and confidence in your supreme faithfulness. Amen.

What is my response to God's promise?

Am I resting in the Lord and trusting Him with my future, my problems, my hopes and dreams? ____________________________

What do I, specifically, need to entrust to Him today?_______

____

____

____

What evidence have I seen in my life that God keeps His promises? ____

____

____

____

Promise Confirmation: Psalm 91:14-16, Psalm 145:13, Isaiah 55:11, Matthew 11:28-30, Hebrews 10:23

__Day 38__

Fellowship in Truth

Psalm 145:17-18

"*The LORD is righteous in all his ways and loving toward all he has made.*

The LORD is near to all who call on him, to all who call on him in truth."

__Promise:__ God promises to be near to *all* who call on Him in truth.

Have you ever told yourself that God doesn't care nor pay attention to what you say and do? This could not be further from the truth. God knows you, for He created you. He loves you. He is just and righteous in His dealing with you. God promises to be with you and be near to you, if you will but ask Him, truthfully, for help. He knows your heart and wants you to respond to Him in truth.

__Lessons and Truths:__

1.   God is accessible.

2.   God is righteous in character and loving in actions toward me.

3.   God desires truth from me.

4.   God wants to have a close relationship with me.

Prayer: Lord, you are holy and righteous and demand that I respond to you in truth. Show me the lies that I am harboring in my life, that I may be full of your grace and truth. Create in me a clean heart, pure, and truthful so that I may draw near to you and communicate with you in total honesty. Amen.

What is my response to God's promise?

Am I truthful in my prayers and thoughts toward God? What do I need to honestly talk to God about today? _________________

____

____

____

What am I facing that I need Him to be near me? ___________

____

____

____

Promise Confirmation: Psalm 116:1-7, John 4:24, Romans 10:8-13. Hebrews 10:22

Day 39

Essential Connection

John 15:5

"*I am the vine; you are the branches. Whoever abides in me and I in him, he it is that bears much fruit, for apart from me you can do nothing.*"

Promise: God promises that abiding in Christ will lead to a fruitful life.

I have a grape vine that grows on an arbor in my back yard. Often, I sit and look at it, marveling at its growth and the fruit that springs up amongst the leaves. It seems like overnight it sprouts and overtakes the arbor. God wants and promises that kind of growing in Him, if we will stay attached to Jesus. Abiding in Christ is a lifelong business that requires concentrated effort on my part. I have to read and study God's Word, pray, and stay connected to other believers. Remaining joined to Jesus is the key to a productive life!

<u>**Lessons and Truths**</u>:

1. Jesus, the vine, is the source of life for believers.
2. The way to connect with God is through Jesus.
3. To bear fruit in our lives (love, joy, peace, patience, kindness, goodness, faithfulness, gentleness and self-control), we must walk with Jesus daily.
4. Without God, nothing that holds any eternal value can be accomplished.

<u>**Prayer**</u>: Lord Jesus, I want to live a life abiding in you. Lead me to a deeper faith that hungers to know you more fully. Cause my faith to grow and produce fruit for you. Use me for your glory and to accomplish your work. Amen.

<u>**What is my response to God's promise?**</u>

What am I doing each day to abide in Jesus? ______________

____

____

What evidence of God's fruit am I seeing in my life? ________

____

____

____

<u>**Promise Confirmation**</u>: Psalm 91, Matthew 19:26, John 15:9-11, Galatians 5:22-23, Ephesians 5:6-10, 1 John 4:13-16

<u>Day 40</u>

Lighten Your Load

Matthew 11:28-30

"Come to me, all who labor and are heavy laden, and I will give you rest. Take my yoke upon you, and learn from me, for I am gentle and lowly in heart, and you will find rest for your souls. For my yoke is easy, and my burden is light."

<u>Promise</u>: God promises rest for my soul, knowledge and gentleness, if I will believe in Jesus and follow Him.

The Jewish followers of Jesus' day were burdened by the legalistic rules of the law. Jesus offered them freedom from the law, as they struggled to fulfill them and earn a place in heaven. Jesus offers us the same freedom from "religious trappings" by requiring only simple faith in Him. Those who seek Jesus will receive eternal rest and salvation, knowledge of God and heavenly things, and God's gentle touch. Jesus promises that His way is not burdensome or hard to bear, but will sustain us and give us rest. All we have to do is come to Him. Today, seek Him in the midst of your busy day and look for His rest to come upon you just as He promised.

Lessons and Truths:

1. God desires that I come to Him through Jesus.
2. God rewards those who come to Him in faith with eternal life, intimate knowledge of Himself and a gentleness of spirit.
3. My yoke of faith in Jesus binds me to Him. He helps me carry my worries and troubles, making them lighter.

Prayer: Lord, thank you that Jesus carries my burdens and walks beside me to give me strength and comfort. Come to me, as I study your Word and pray, that I may know you personally and learn your ways. Teach me how to please you and find rest in Jesus. Amen.

What is my response to God's promise?

What am I doing to learn more about Jesus? _________________

____

What benefits from a close walk with Jesus am I seeing in my life? ____

____

Do I have peace, increasing knowledge of God, a lighter spirit, hope? ____

____

Promise Confirmation: Psalm 23, Psalm 51:10-12, Proverbs19:23, Jeremiah 6:16a, Galatians 5:22-23, 1 John 5:3-5

Day 41

Disappointment? Not Possible!

Isaiah 49:22-23

"*This is what the Sovereign LORD says: 'See, I will beckon to the Gentiles, I will lift up my banner to the peoples; they will bring your sons in their arms and carry your daughters on their shoulders. Kings will be your foster fathers, and their queens your nursing mothers. They will bow down before you with their faces to the ground; they will lick the dust at your feet. Then you will know that I am the LORD; those who hope in me will not be disappointed.'*"

Promises: 1. God promised to return the children of Israel from their captivity in Babylon, which was fulfilled with the help of pagan kings, as God promised (Ezra 1). 2. God promises all believers that hope in Him will never lead to disappointment.

How do you handle disappointment? Do you pout, cry, yell, blame others or do you look to God for help? The best way to handle disappointment is it to give the problem, or situation, to God before the results are known. Pray before you have the results and leave it to God. Giving it to God before it is all said-and-done, allows you to accept God's work. It will increase your faith and trust in Him, as He works in, and through, your circumstances. This promise provides hope to all believers. He is sovereign and has the best plans for us. We just need to trust Him!

<u>Lessons and Truths</u>:
1. God's Word has many layers of messages to his people, then and now.
2. God is sovereign over all peoples and nations.
3. Hope placed in God will always bring positive results.
4. God wants the best for me and doesn't want to see me disappointed.
5. Faith in God brings me hope.

<u>Prayer</u>: Lord, you are sovereign and have all circumstances under your control. Increase my faith so I will not doubt this. Help me to put my trust in you for the details of my life. I know that you only want good for me. Thank you for the hope and assurance this brings to me each day. Amen.

<u>What is my response to God's promise?</u>

Where is my hope in my own ability and not with God? _____

____

What is causing me disappointment that I need to give to you, Lord?_______________________________________

____

<u>Promise Confirmation</u>: Psalm 25:1-5, Psalm 62:5-8, Isaiah 40:28-31, Romans 5:1-5, Hebrews 10:22-23

Day 42

Godly Restoration

Joel 2:25-27

"*I will repay you for the years the locusts have eaten—the great locust and the young locust, the other locusts and the locust swarm—my great army that I sent among you. You will have plenty to eat, until you are full, and you will praise the name of the LORD your God, who has worked wonders for you; never again will my people be shamed. Then you will know that I am in Israel, that I am the LORD your God, and that there is no other; never again will my people be shamed.*"

Promise: God promises restoration in my life from the damage done by locusts. Locusts can be problems brought on by my own sin or calamity brought upon me through a sinful world.

I love this verse and have quoted it many times. It shows God's love toward those who belong to Him. Just as He promised and delivered restoration to the Israelites, after their many problems brought on by their sin and circumstances, God will do the same for me. During difficult times in my life, it has felt as though I would never get beyond my problems. However, as I look back, I now see how God restored me and brought me way beyond the hurt and devastation. Godly restoration does not "fix" a situation and make it like it was before. His restoration brings about new life and purpose. God truly restores us from the inside out. The more I experience godly restoration in my life, the more assured I am that God loves and cares for me!

<u>Lessons and Truths</u>:
1. God is merciful and brings restoration.
2. God can and does work wonders on our behalf.
3. God is the one and only God.
4. God's promises are eternal.

<u>Prayer:</u> Lord, I know that many of the calamities in my life are brought on by my own sinful and willful behavior. Reveal to me my sinful ways that I may repent and seek your forgiveness and restoration. I know that you are working in my life and want only good for me. Increase my faith and trust in you so that I will look to you for guidance and provision, instead of the world around me. Amen.

<u>What is my response to God's promise</u>?

Where do I need godly restoration in my life? ______________

____

____

____

<u>Promise Confirmation:</u> Psalm 23, Psalm 147:2-6, 1 Peter 2:24-25, 1 Peter 5:10

Day 43

Generous Hearts Needed

Luke 6:38

"Give, and it will be given to you. A good measure, pressed down, shaken together and running over, will be poured into your lap. For with the measure you use, it will be measured to you."

Promise: Jesus promises if I give generously, it will be returned to me in even *greater* measure.

This godly principle of giving is based on our faith in God's goodness. We may not see the return on our investment for days, weeks, or even years. We have to trust that God will return our investment to us in abundance. This means our return will be greater than what we gave (monetarily, time, or good deeds). God is gracious and knows our character. He knows that if every time we give, we get something in return, the only reason we will continue to give will be to get. Our Christian giving needs to be motivated by our love for God. We need to trust God that our reward will be a good measure, pressed down and running over, just as He has promised. If you are a Christian, you know this principle is true. You can never out give God!

Lessons and Truths:
1. Giving is needed to receive.
2. Giving of time, talent, money, etc. to God and His purposes is always rewarded.
3. God's return is packed, overflowing and poured out on the giver.
4. If you give sparingly, with a stingy heart, you will receive sparingly.

Prayer: Father, you have created us to give and serve. Show me ways I can be generous today toward those I meet. Give me your eyes to see their need and the right measure to give to them. Hold me accountable for my giving and open my heart to be generous and loving. Protect my mind from the "give to get" philosophy. Let me see ways to give of myself, my time, and my talents that will be pleasing to you. Amen.

What is my response to God's promise?

What is my heart attitude towards giving? _______________________

____

____

What ways do I give generously to God and His work?________

____

Promise Confirmation: Proverbs 11:24-25, Matthew 7:9-12, Acts 20:35, 2 Corinthians 9:6-8

Day 44

God's Comfort

Hebrews 13:5-8

"*Keep your lives free from the love of money and be content with what you have, because God has said, 'Never will I leave you; never will I forsake you,' So we say with confidence, 'The Lord is my helper; I will not be afraid. What can man do to me?' Remember your leaders, who spoke the word of God to you. Consider the outcome of their way of life and imitate their faith. Jesus Christ is the same yesterday and today and forever.*"

Promise: God promises He will not leave me or abandon me. He will help me and keep me from being afraid. God is unchanging for all eternity.

This promise has many layers that comfort me. I do not need to fear for a lack of resources nor love. I do not need to fret over helplessness nor fear what others may say or do to me. God promises that *He will stand with me and provide me with all that I need.* Knowing this truth brings contentment. I know God will do what He promised. In addition, He promises that He will never change. We live in a world of constant change. We learn to live and survive through being flexible. God says He is immutable—or unchanging. Doesn't knowing that God is always there, and will always be there, bring you great assurance? He is constant and I can always count on Him!

<u>Lessons and Truths</u>:
1. God is immutable, unchanging.
2. God is faithful and will always provide for me.
3. God desires to help me and keep me from living in fear.
4. God's ways provide contentment in the midst of a sin-filled world.

<u>Prayer</u>: Lord, you are the Almighty, Sovereign Lord who brings contentment to my life. Your ways are perfect and will lead me away from fear. Give me peace that comes from knowing Jesus and guide me to seek His help each day. Increase my faith so that I may serve you with assurance and glorify you daily. Amen.

<u>What is my response to God's promise?</u>

What do I need God's help with today? _______________________

____

____

How does knowing God is immutable assure me? ___________

____

____

<u>Promise Confirmation</u>:   Psalm 46:1-3, Matthew 28:19-20, Philippians 4:11-13, Hebrews 10:23, James 1:17

Day 45

Stillness and Patience Required

Psalm 37:7-9

"Be still before the LORD and wait patiently for him; fret not yourself over the one who prospers in his way, over the man who carries out evil devices! Refrain from anger, and forsake wrath! Fret not yourself; it tends only to evil. For the evildoers shall be cut off, but those who wait for the LORD shall inherit the land."

Promise: God promises to take care of evildoers and asks me to be still and wait patiently, trusting Him to provide.

David penned this psalm out from his own experience. He waited fourteen years to be crowned king of Israel after he was anointed by the prophet Samuel. During that time he was pursued and harassed by King Saul, who was out to kill him. He was tempted to seek revenge (see 1 Samuel 24 and 26 for the complete story). David was patient and experienced God's provision and care. David became king of Israel in God's time and not his own. Waiting for God's time is often hard, but these verses caution us that worry and fear will lead to sin. Trust in God alone to resolve your problems, then you will receive His reward.

<u>Lessons and Truths</u>:
1. God is sovereign and knows all the people in my life and their intentions.
2. Following God's way requires patience.
3. God desires that I not worry.
4. God is just and will deal with evil permanently.

<u>Prayer</u>: Father, you know what is best for my life just as you did for your servant David. Keep me focused upon you so that I will not worry or fret about the situations I am facing. Allow me to see the evildoers for what they are and help me refrain from anger. Help me to stand firm against their attacks and grant me patience, as I wait on your timing. Amen.

<u>What is my response to God's promise?</u>

What am I worried about that I need to give to God today?

____

____

Where do I need to follow God's command to be still and wait patiently? ____

____

<u>Promise Confirmation</u>:   Psalm 46:10, Proverbs 24:19-20, Isaiah 55:9, Hebrews 10:30-31

<u>Day 46</u>

Foundation of Truth

Proverbs 30:5-6

"*Every word of God proves true; he is a shield to those who take refuge in him. Do not add to his words, lest he rebuke you and you be found a liar.*"

<u>Promise</u>: God promises that His Word is true, without error, and He will protect anyone who hides in Him.

What better foundation can we have for life than God's Word? He promises that His Word is true, and we can trust *all* of it. Seeking God's refuge, or protected place, does not mean I am hiding from the world. But rather, that He provides a solid foundation, understanding and wisdom, so that I can deal with the world. He wants me to know that His Word is enough and I don't need to worry about there being an important point missing in it. I don't need to keep looking for something else. He has made His Word sufficient for all my needs. Psalm 119:11 reminds us that His Word leads to a godly life: "*I have stored your word in my heart, that I might not sin against you.*" Praise

God today for the truth of His Word and its sustaining power!

<u>Lessons and Truths</u>:
1. God's Word is truth, without error.
2. God is my protector and shield.
3. Seeking refuge in God always results in protection.
4. Trying to add to God's Word will result in being found a liar and lead to rebuke.

<u>Prayer</u>: Father, you have made your Word complete and sufficient for all my needs. Give me your wisdom as I read and study your Word so that I may see and know your truth. Show me the completeness of your Word. Help me not wander or stray from your truths. Thank you, for I can stand firm on your Word and know your peace. Amen.

<u>What is my response to God's promise?</u>

How am I seeking God's refuge and protection? ______________

____

Am I doubting the truthfulness of God's Word? (Write your doubts, *then* ask God to reveal His truth to you through the power of the Holy Spirit). ______________________

____

____

____

<u>Promise Confirmation</u>: Deuteronomy 4:2, Psalm 12:6, Psalm 18:30, Psalm 119:137-144, Matthew 5:18, Matthew 24:35, John 17:17, Hebrews 4:12, Revelation 22:18-20

<u>Day 47</u>

Mountain Moving Faith

Matthew 17:19-20

*"Then the disciples came to Jesus in private and asked, 'Why couldn't we drive it out?' [**It** refers to a demonic spirit living inside a boy in verses 14-18.] He replied, 'Because you have so little faith, I tell you the truth, if you have faith as small as a mustard seed, you can say to this mountain, "Move from here to there" and it will move. Nothing will be impossible for you.'"*

<u>**Promise:**</u> God promises that *great faith* can accomplish *great things*.

When I was a young girl, my father gave me a necklace with a tiny mustard seed inside. I loved looking at it and seeing how small it was. Wearing it, reminded me of this verse and the promise that great faith can do great things. It is not the quantity of my faith but the *quality* that makes the difference. Where are you placing your faith? Is it in your own abilities or in God's power? As you think about this verse today, place your faith in the all-powerful God who is able to accomplish anything, for without Him we can do nothing.

<u>Lessons and Truths:</u>
1.   Faith in God can accomplish the impossible.
2.   God is omnipotent, all powerful.
3.   God gives power to believers.
4.   Even a little *true* faith has great power.

<u>Prayer</u>: Lord, you are the source of all power and the true mover of the mountains I face in my life. Revitalize my faith and bring me to a higher level of trust in you. Use me to accomplish great things in you. Thank you for the visual reminder of the mustard seed and what you *can* and *will* do in my life. Amen.

<u>What is my response to God's promise?</u>

How am I using my faith? ____

____

Am I moving mountains or just stirring up dust?_______________

____

____

Where do I see things requiring mountain-moving faith in my life? ____

____

____

<u>Promise Confirmation</u>: Joshua 23:14, John 14:12-14, Acts 1:8, Ephesians 2:8-10

<u>Day 48</u>

Joyful Encounters

James 1:2-4

"Count it all joy, my brothers, when you meet trials of various kinds, for you know that the testing of your faith produces steadfastness. And let steadfastness have its full effect, that you may be perfect and complete, lacking in nothing."

<u>Promise</u>: God promises that trials that test my faith produce steadfastness and completeness.

As I reflected upon this promise, I needed a description of this steadfastness I get from persevering in Christ throughout the trials of life. The dictionary defines *steadfastness* as the ability to stand firm, unswerving, constant, and resolute in faith. When I am tempted to waver in my faith, God promises standing firm with Christ will result in my being perfect, complete, and lacking in nothing. I needed this today, as it gives me assurance that true victory and fulfillment is only found when I stand with Christ. His blessing of completeness and perfection is far beyond anything I could ever gain on earth, and it is found only through Christ Jesus.

<u>**Lessons and Truths:**</u>

1. God wants me to endure faith tests with joy, as they are proof of His love and desire to hone and shape my character.
2. God allows trials in my life so that I will become more firmly rooted and resolute in my faith.
3. Faith tests result in bringing God's perfection and blessing into my life.

<u>**Prayer:**</u> Lord, help me to see the trails I face today as an opportunity to grow in my faith. Help me to keep your joy in all circumstances and share it with the people I meet. Help me see though your eyes and look for what you would have me accomplish. Give me your grace to be humble, caring, and loving toward others. Make me a firm witness to those around me, so that they may know that I stand for Christ. Amen.

<u>What is my response to God's promise?</u>

What is my attitude towards trials of faith? Am I persevering with joy in Christ or am I approaching the trial with bitterness and sorrow? ____

____

Where do I need to persevere with joy today? _______________

____

Where do I need to eliminate bitterness or sorrow? __________

____

<u>**Promise Confirmation:**</u> Psalm 66:8-12, 2 Corinthians 8:1-5, 1 Peter 1:6-7, 1 Peter 4:12-14

<u>Day 49</u>

Perfect Peace

Isaiah 26:3-4

"You keep him in perfect peace whose mind is stayed on you, because he trusts in you. Trust in the Lord forever, for the LORD GOD is an everlasting rock."

<u>Promise</u>: God promises His peace when I trust and stay focused on Him.

How hard is it to stay focused on God during my busy week and not be drawn into worldly concerns and pursuits? It is really hard. It takes diligence to stay in God's Word each day, pray often, and be open to the leading of the Holy Spirit. However, God promises perfect peace if I seek to follow this path. God's peace eliminates worry, discouragement, fear, hopelessness, disappointment, and gives me purpose in serving Him. God makes the prize of peace well worth the effort, as His rewards are for now and into eternity.

<u>**Lessons and Truths**</u>:

1. God can give me peace.
2. I need to trust Him and stay focused.
3. God is eternal, therefore I can trust Him forever.
4. God is steadfast, an eternal foundation for my faith.

Prayer: Lord, you are eternal and totally trustworthy. You are the giver of perfect peace. Help me to stay focused on you, through your Word and prayer, so that I can serve you fully. Let my life glorify you and give me your peace. Amen.

<u>**What is my response to your promise**</u>?

When have I experienced God's perfect peace? ____________

____

____

What is blocking that perfect peace in my life today? ________

____

____

Where do I need to trust God more fully? __________________

____

____

____

Promise Confirmation: Psalm 112:6-7, Psalm 119:165, John 14:27, John 16:33, Philippians 4:6-7, James 1:2-4

<u>Day 50</u>

Joy and Strength

Nehemiah 8:9-10

"*And Nehemiah, who was the governor, and Ezra the priest and scribe, and the Levites who taught the people said to all the people, 'This day is holy to the LORD your God; do not mourn or weep.' For all the people wept as they heard the words of the Law. Then he said to them, 'Go your way. Eat the fat and drink sweet wine, and send portions to anyone who has nothing ready, for this day is holy to our Lord. And do not be grieved, for the joy of the LORD is your strength.'*"

<u>Promise</u>: God promises joy and strength when we are grieved over our sin and repent from it.

What is your reaction to hearing God's Word? Do you apply His Word to your life and consider your actions? Are you grieved when you see that you are sinning and not living as God would have you live? Nehemiah encouraged the children of Israel, as they heard God's Word, to recognize their sin and move forward with Him. God promises His strength and joy to *all* who desire to walk in His ways. This is a wonderful reassurance that God supports and encourages you in your walk with Him!

Lessons and Truths:
1. God's Word has power to affect me when I hear it.
2. Grieving and repenting over sin puts me in a position to receive God's strength.
3. God is the source of joy and strength for living.

Prayer: Lord, allow your Holy Spirit to convict me of sin in my life. Help me to repent and turn anew, so that I may walk with you. Direct my way through your Word that my joy may be complete. Strengthen me so that I may stand firm on your Word and glorify you. Amen.

What is my response to God's promise?

Where do I need to repent from sin? _______________________

____

How do I react to hearing or studying God's Word? __________

____

How am I experiencing God's joy and strength in my life? ____

____

____

Promise Confirmation: Psalm 30:8-12, Psalm 119: 9-16, John 15:7-11, Acts 3:19

Day 51

Pure, Godly Love

John 3:16

"*For God so loved the world, that he gave his only Son, that whoever believes in him should not perish but have eternal life.*"

Promise: God promises eternal life to those who believe in Jesus.

What promises do you make to your loved ones? Do your promises lead you to show kindness and your great care for them? God showed us the greatest example of love when He sent Jesus to give up His life up for us. His sacrifice allowed us to be in a right relationship with God and be eternally free from the bondage of sin. Imagine the anguish the Father must have felt to see His Son, Jesus, suffer such an excruciating death. It is beyond comprehension. God's love has no end. It is eternal. Talk to your family and friends today about His great love.

<u>Lessons and Truths</u>:

1. God's motivation for saving me is LOVE.
2. Faith in Jesus has eternal benefits.
3. Providing for my salvation brought about Christ's suffering and death.
4. Without faith in Jesus, death would be both physical and spiritual.

<u>Prayer</u>: God, thank you for sending Jesus to die for my sins. Thank you that faith in Jesus allows me to love you and receive your mercy and forgiveness. I desire to know you more fully and trust in your faithfulness. You have shown me unmerited favor through faith in your Son, Jesus, and I know I will live with you eternally. Amen.

<u>What is my response to God's promise?</u>

Do I believe in Jesus and His power to save me?__________

____

____

*If you do not know Jesus personally, be sure to look up and pray over the **confirmation** verses today. Settle your future for eternity.*

Who can I tell about God's love today? ________________

____

____

<u>Promise Confirmation</u>: John 3:35-36, John 5:24, John 6:40, 44-51, 1 John 5:1, 5, 10-12

<u>Day 52</u>

Living Hope

1 Peter 1:3-5

"Praise be to the God and Father of our Lord Jesus Christ! In his great mercy he has given us new birth into a living hope through the resurrection of Jesus Christ from the dead, and into an inheritance that can never perish, spoil or fade—kept in heaven for you, who through faith are shielded by God's power until the coming of the salvation that is ready to be revealed in the last time."

<u>Promise</u>: God promises a living hope through Jesus' resurrection—an eternal—non-perishable inheritance that is shielded by God's power and an assurance of Jesus' return.

Wow! My hope in God is living because Jesus conquered death and rose from the dead! Since He is alive, it makes my salvation imperishable and good for eternity. The salvation I received when I accepted Jesus as my Savior is protected from that time forward by God's power until all is done and Jesus returns. This gives me confidence and assurance that my faith is solid and cannot be taken away, and God, himself, is shielding and protecting me through my faith in Jesus. What a powerful promise!

<u>Lessons and Truths</u>:
1. God is merciful.
2. God gives me eternal living hope for my future through Christ's resurrection.
3. God has an inheritance for me as a believer in Jesus.
4. This inheritance, my salvation, from God is protected and shielded by His power.

<u>Prayer</u>: Lord, you are full of mercy and your plans for my future cannot be thwarted. You know the good things you have planned for my life and you give me a living hope. Thank you for sending Jesus to die for my sins, so that I can live with you for eternity. Your gift of salvation, through Jesus, is protected by your power. Help me to live with confidence fully trusting you to keep that which you have given me safe. Amen.

<u>What is my response to God's promise?</u>

How have I experienced God's mercy? ________________________

____

What differences do I see in my life because of my living hope — Jesus? ____

____

____

<u>Promise Confirmation</u>: Psalm 91:1-4, Psalm 119:114, Isaiah 51:6, Acts 4:12, Titus 1:2-3, I Peter 1:3-9

<u>Day 53</u>

God's Preservation

Psalm 145:19-20

"He fulfills the desires of those who fear him; he also hears their cry and saves them. The LORD preserves all who love him, but all the wicked he will destroy."

Promise: God promises to fulfill my desires, hear my cry, preserve and save me, if I will fear and love Him.

What does it take to **show** God that you love and fear him? God tells us in 1 Samuel 15:22: *"To obey is better than sacrifice."* Being obedient to God's Word and showing reverence for who He is will help you to glorify Him in all you say and do. Jesus said in Luke 10:27: *"'Love the Lord your God with all your heart and with all your soul and with all your strength and with all your mind.' and 'Love your neighbor as yourself.'"* Loving God and fearing Him means making Him #1 in your life. This will lead you to treat others with more kindness, tolerance, and patience. God's promised rewards of preservation, salvation, accessibility, and love are beyond anything we can even imagine or grasp! Praise Him!

Lessons and Truths:

1. God is accessible and He hears my cries.
2. God is sovereign as all creation is under His control.
3. God saves.
4. God desires that I praise, adore, and love Him.
5. God preserves and keeps those who love Him safe from eternal destruction.
6. Not loving and fearing God results in destruction and death.

Prayer: Lord, I desire to love you more dearly and walk closer to you each day. Help me to be responsive to your leading and open to your correction. I am so thankful that you watch over me and that I can call on you at any time. Be with me today as I interact with others, that they may see your love though me. Amen

What is my response to God's promise?

How am I showing God that I love and fear Him? _________

____

____

What is the desire of my heart that I would ask of God? _____

____

____

Promise Confirmation: Deuteronomy 6:4-9, Psalm 147:7-11, John 3:16, John 14:15, 21, Hebrews 4:16, Hebrews 7:25, Hebrews 10:37-39

<u>Day 54</u>

Spotless Before God

Isaiah 1:18-20

"'Come now, let us reason together,' says the LORD. 'Though your sins are like scarlet, they shall be as white as snow; though they are red as crimson, they shall be like wool. If you are willing and obedient, you will eat the best from the land; but if you resist and rebel, you will be devoured by the sword.' For the mouth of the LORD has spoken."

<u>**Promise:**</u> God promises to cleanse and forgive my sins and that obedience to Him will bring about blessings. Likewise, living in sin with a disobedient, unrepentant heart will result in death.

This is one of my favorite visuals of God's cleansing power and forgiveness. Through Jesus' work on the cross, I can be forgiven and presented clean and pure before God, like snow or wool. This is a powerful reminder that refusing to follow God's ways, and living with a heart filled with disobedience and resistance, leads to spiritual death. God promises following Him will result in the very best for me, and I will be blessed. I know that holding on to sin, nurturing and feeding into depression, resentment, hatred, and fear will cause my heart to harden and turn away from God. Will you open your heart to Him today and be clean?

Lessons and Truths:

1. God can and does forgive sin and makes me clean.
2. God desires for me to have a willing and obedient heart.
3. The consequence of rejecting God results in spiritual death.
4. God blesses those who follow Him.

Prayer: Lord, you are so loving and gracious to me. You sent Jesus to die for my sins so that I can come to you pure and spotless. I did nothing to deserve this. Forgive my sins and create in me a clean heart that I may reflect your glory and be used by you in a mighty way. Guard my heart that I may obediently follow and walk with you. Amen.

What is my response to God's promise?

Where do I see myself as willing and obedient?________________

____

____

Where do I need to seek God's forgiveness for today?__________

____

____

Promise Confirmation: Psalm 51:1-2, Romans 2:5-11, Romans 3:23, Romans 5:18-19, 1 Peter 3:9-12, 1 John 1:8-10

Day 55

Kingdom Priorities

Luke 12:29-31

"And do not seek what you are to eat and what you are to drink, nor be worried. For all the nations of the world seek after these things, and your Father knows that you need them. Instead, seek his kingdom, and these things will be added to you."

Promise: God promises to meet our physical and emotional needs if we will seek His kingdom before worldly pursuits.

This promise helps me to keep my worries about worldly needs in perspective. How much time is wasted worrying about meeting my bills or what I will do *if* something happens? The time could be better used studying God's Word, volunteering to help others, or speaking about God and His love for me. God wants me focused, with eternal priorities, not dwelling on the temporal things of life. I need to trust Him to meet my needs and keep my focus on Him!

<u>Lessons and Truths</u>:

1. God is sovereign and things of the world are totally within His control.

2. God does not want me to worry about my needs.

3. God wants me to focus on Him and things in His kingdom—salvation, righteousness, holiness, and fruits of the Spirit.

4. Setting and pursuing godly goals = God's provision for all my needs, both physically and emotionally.

<u>Prayer</u>: Lord, give me your perspective on the things that surround me and keep me focused on you. Help me to put aside temporal worries, which have a tendency to overwhelm and consume me from day to day. Give me a desire to pursue your kingdom and righteousness. Increase my faith and trust in you so that I may be used for your glory. Amen.

What is my response to God's promise?

What proof am I seeing in my life of my pursing God's kingdom?

____

____

Where do I need to re-prioritize my thinking to better align with seeking His purposes?_____________________________________

____

____

____

Promise Confirmation: Psalm 34:8-10, Matthew 6:7-13, Philippians 4:19, Hebrews 11:6

<u>Day 56</u>

Soul Food

John 6:35

"Then Jesus declared, 'I am the bread of life. He who comes to me will never go hungry, and he who believes in me will never be thirsty.'"

<u>**Promise:**</u> God promises faith in Jesus is life and food for my soul.

We all know that our bodies need food and water to live, but our spiritual soul also needs food and water. This is the substance that Jesus is talking about here. He is the only one that can feed our spirit. Jesus gives us nourishment through His Word, assurance though the Holy Spirit, and hope for eternity through His death and resurrection. He frees us from the power of sin giving life to our body and spirit. His food and drink are totally complete, lacking in nothing. Be sure you partake of His food today.

<u>**Lessons and Truths:**</u>

1. Faith is the pipeline to my soul, bringing me nourishment.
2. Jesus provides food and living water through faith, which gives promised salvation for eternity.
3. God provides all we need through Jesus. He is the God who is enough—Jehovah Jireh.
4. God is eternal.

<u>**Prayer:**</u> Lord Jesus, you have all that I need. You know my inner most thoughts and desires. You know that which I need to make me whole and complete. Give me eyes to see your provision and a grateful heart for all those things you bring into my life to strengthen my walk and buildup my character. Thank you for being my all in all. Amen.

<u>**What is my response to God's promise?**</u>

How am I allowing the Holy Spirit to feed me?_____________

____

____

Where am I trying to do things myself instead of letting God provide for my needs? _____________________________

____

____

<u>**Promise Confirmation:**</u> Matthew 4:2-4, Luke 12: 27-31, John 4:13-14, John 7:37-39,   Hebrews 5:12-14

<u>Day 57</u>

Newness in Life

Ezekiel 36:25-27

"*I will sprinkle clean water on you, and you shall be clean from all your uncleanness, and from all your idols I will cleanse you. And I will give you a new heart, and a new spirit I will put within you. And I will remove the heart of stone from your flesh and give you a heart of flesh. And I will put my Spirit within you, and cause you to walk in my statues and be careful to obey my rules.*"

<u>Promise</u>: God promises to remove my sin and create in me a new heart. He will also put His Spirit within me to help me walk in obedience to Him.

This is a precious promise that the Lord and Creator of the universe gives to each of us who know and love Him. We know it is true, as His Word cannot be thwarted or changed. He does not change His mind. When God says, "I Will", He means it and is faithful to do as He promised. He will remove all my sins and bury them in the deepest sea. He will create in me a new and clean heart. With the indwelling of the Holy Spirit, I can walk with Jesus each day and depend upon Him to uphold and guide me. Praise God!

Lessons and Truths:

1. God can and does forgive my sins.
2. God can and does create a new being within me that is alive by His Spirit.
3. God desires obedience.
4. Sin and disobedience will separate me from God.

Prayer: Lord, I desire a relationship with you. I confess my sinful nature and ask for a clean heart that is obedient to you. Fill me with your Spirit and walk beside me each day. Cause me to lean upon you and seek your guidance as I meet the trials and temptations of life. Keep me in your Word that I may learn your ways and wholly walk in them. Amen.

What is my response to God's promise?

What sins do I need to confess and repent of today? _________

____

____

How do I see God's Spirit at work in my life? ____________

____

____

Promise Confirmation: Psalm 51:10-12, Micah 7:18-20, 2 Corinthians 5:17, Ephesians 5:8-11, Hebrews 10:22-23

Day 58

Purpose Guaranteed

Isaiah 55:10-11

"As the rain and the snow come down from heaven, and do not return to it without watering the earth and making it bud and flourish, so that it yields seed for the sower and bread for the eater, so is my word that goes out from my mouth: It will not return to me empty, but will accomplish what I desire and achieve the purpose for which I sent it."

Promise: God promises when His Word is sent out (told, read, preached, etc.), it will not come back without results. It will accomplish and achieve what God intended.

I find this promise so encouraging. Here, God says that when we are working in ministry, speaking God's truths, He is guarantees results. He knows the purpose and fruit that will be produced. Even if we can't see it, this verse guarantees that God knows and will produce the desired result. We just need to keep sharing His truth and let Him see it through to completion.

<u>**Lessons and Truths:**</u>

1. Just like the rain nurtures the earth and produces results, God intends for His Word to feed, nourish, and produce fruit in me.
2. God's Word is always productive.
3. God's Word achieves God's will; His intended purpose.
4. God's Word will accomplish His work.

<u>**Prayer:**</u> Lord, help me to be diligent in studying your Word and consistent in applying your truths to my life. You promise that your Word in me will lead to good results. Open my eyes that I may see a glimpse of that good fruit in my life and experience the wonder of your transforming power. Amen.

<u>**What is my response to God's promise?**</u>

How can I share God's Word with others more effectively?

____

____

How am I allowing God's Word to work in my heart and life as I study Scripture? _______________________________

____

____

____

<u>**Promise Confirmation:**</u> Psalm 119: 9, 11, 105, Isaiah 46:8-10, Romans 8: 28-30, 2 Corinthians 9:10-11, Philippians 2:13

<u>Day 59</u>

The Perfect Gate

John 10:9-10

"*I am the gate; whoever enters through me will be saved. He will come in and go out, and find pasture. The thief comes only to steal and kill and destroy; I have come that you may have life, and have it to the full.*"

<u>Promise</u>: God promises Jesus is the way (gate) to salvation and a full life.

Some people still have old fashioned gates leading to their property or their front door. To enter their house you have to unlock the gate and walk through to get inside. If you don't pass through the gate, you can't get into their yard to see and greet those inside. This is the visual image that Jesus explains through this verse. He is the gateway, the door, to having a relationship with God. Belief in Jesus provides you with an entry into His kingdom and a life that is full and holds eternal rewards. What a beautiful, welcoming picture this gives you. Not only does He greet you, but rewards you with eternity and fullness of life! Thank you, Jesus.

Lessons and Truths:

1. God provides the way for me to be saved though His son, Jesus.
2. Those opposing God seek to steal, kill, and destroy.
3. God desires good for me and a life that is totally full.

Prayer: Thank you God for sending Jesus to die for my sins so that I can have a relationship with you. Only you could provide the perfect Savior to redeem and provide me with eternal life. Only you could promise me a full life, through faith in Jesus. Help me to stand firm in my faith and be, totally, committed to you, trusting you to fill my life with your love, purpose, and direction. I want to glorify you. Give me a desire to tell others about Jesus and His redeeming power. Amen.

What is my response to God's promise?

Where am I trying to seek my own way? ___________________

____

____

Where can I see God's fullness in my life? ________________

____

____

Promise Confirmation: Psalm 98:1-3, John 14:6, Acts 4:12, Romans 10:9-13, Ephesians 3:14-19, Revelation 3:20

<u>Day 60</u>

Peace of Mind

John 14:27

"*Peace I leave with you; my peace I give you. I do not give to you as the world gives. Do not let your hearts be troubled and do not be afraid.*"

Promise: God promises to give me His peace, which will leave my heart untroubled and unafraid.

This promise is a great comfort at any time. You don't have to be going through hard times, facing death, or struggling with emotional trauma to claim this verse. Each day brings its own trials, knowing that you can rest in His peace each the day, brings great comfort. During times of uncertainty, you can cling to this verse and know that God will calm you and guide. You will experience a peace that passes all worldly understanding. Praise God for His grace and sufficiency! He knows exactly what you need, just ask Him!

<u>**Lessons and Truths:**</u>

1. God gives peace.
2. God desires that I trust in Him so I can be without fear and have an untroubled heart.
3. God is compassionate.
4. God is sovereign over all matters in my life.
5. Fear and trouble do not come from God.

<u>**Prayer:**</u> Lord, hold me in your hand today and allow your peace to penetrate my entire being. Help me to cling to this promise, knowing that you are fully capable of delivering peace 24/7 wherever I am. Thank you for your care, love, and desire for me to live in peace, as I trust in your sovereignty. Amen.

<u>**What is my response to God's promise?**</u>

When do I seek God's peace? _______________________________

____

____

____

Where do I need God's peace today? ____________________

____

____

____

<u>**Promise Confirmation:**</u>   Psalm 29:11, Isaiah 26:3-4, John 16:33, Galatians 5:22-23, Philippians 4:6-7

<u>Day 61</u>

Total Support

Isaiah 41: 9-10

"*I took you from the ends of the earth, from its farthest corners I called you. I said, 'You are my servant', I have chosen you and have not rejected you. So do not fear, for I am with you; do not be dismayed, for I am your God. I will strengthen you and help you; I will uphold you with my righteous right hand.*"

<u>Promise</u>: God chose me and promises to be my God. He will always be with me, strengthen, help, and uphold me through Christ.

The children of Israel were God's chosen people and were facing impending exile to Babylon due to their sinfulness. Isaiah gave words of encouragement that would help them realize that God was there with them. As New Testament Christians we are also chosen by God and will receive this same encouragement, strength, and help through our faith in Christ. God calls Jesus His righteous right hand, which shows His place of honor and immediate accessibility to God— the Father. God is emphatic about His role in our lives as He says, *"I **will** strengthen, help* *and uphold you.*" With God nothing is impossible, we just need to have faith and lean upon Him as we live each day.

Lessons and Truths:

1. God choses those who follow Him.
2. God is omnipresent and always with me.
3. God has abundant strength so He can strengthen me.
4. God personally helps His creation.
5. God provided Christ to uphold me through His saving work on the cross.
6. God's presence in my life dispels fear.

Prayer: Father God, how can I ever express my thankfulness to you for choosing me to be yours? Through faith in your Son, Jesus, I can know your protection, love, and care. Your arms are always around me. You guide my steps and hold me up in times of distress and need. Your indwelling Holy Spirt allows me to be strong and live my life without fear. Guide me today and open doors for me to boldly tell others about the wondrous things you do for me. Amen.

What is my response to God's promise?

Where do I need God's strength, presence, and uplifting today?

____

What fear am I facing that I need to give to God? ___________

____

Promise Confirmation: Deuteronomy 31:6, Psalm 98:1-2, Psalm 118:13-14, Isaiah 43:1-3a, Habakkuk 3:17-19, Matthew 28:19-20, John 15:16, Ephesians 1:11-14, Philippians 4:12-13, 2 Thessalonians 2:13-14, Hebrews 13:5-6

Day 62

Hope-filled Calling

Psalm 86:5-7

"You are forgiving and good, O Lord, abounding in love to all who call to you. Hear my prayer, O LORD; listen to my cry for mercy. In the day of my trouble I will call to you, for you will answer me."

Promise: God promises to answer my calls for help and mercy.

When you are in trouble who do you call? If you have leaking pipes you call a plumber, if shingles are missing, you call a roofer, and if your car breaks down you call a mechanic. What about in your life? When you have emotional stresses in relationships, suffer from depression, loneliness, financial difficulties, complications in schedules, disappointments or have problems at work, do you turn to God? God is omniscient, all-knowing. He knows our problems before we even ask. When we turn to Him and ask for mercy and help, this verse assures us that He will hear, and He will answer! Praise God!!

<u>**Lessons and Truths**</u>:

1. God is accessible.
2. I can rely on God to answer me.
3. God demands my participation; I must call upon Him.
4. God's response will be loving and merciful.
5. God is forgiving and good.

Prayer: Thank you, Lord for the assurance these verses bring. I can call upon you and know you will answer my prayer. Help me to trust in your timing and wait for your answer, whether it is yes, no, or be still and wait. I know you are loving, forgiving, and merciful. I know that you know exactly what I need. Give me your peace, as I wait upon you. Amen.

<u>**What is my response to God's promise?**</u>

How often and for what or whom do I usually pray? _________

____

What am I *not* praying for because I am afraid of God's answer?

____

____

David wrote that God is abounding in love, forgiveness, mercy, and trustworthiness. Where have I experienced this in my life?

____

____

____

Promise Confirmation: Psalm 121, Lamentations 3:25-26, Hebrews 4:16, 1 Peter 5:6-11

Day 63

Living Forgiven

1 Peter 2:24

"*He himself bore our sins in his body on the tree, that we might die to sin and live to righteousness. By his wounds you have been healed.*"

Promise: God promises that through Jesus' death on the cross my sins have been forgiven and I can live a righteous life in Him.

Often, when I am serving the cup for communion I say *"and with his stripes we are healed"* (Isaiah 53:5b). The thought that my sins are forgiven because of Christ's suffering on the cross is a sobering thought. He did not sin, but took all of mankind's sin upon Himself so that we could be clean and able to come into a relationship with the Father. Because of His death, we have the Holy Spirit to indwell us and give us the power to live a righteous life, pleasing to God. Thank you, Lord Jesus.

<u>**Lessons and Truths:**</u>

1. Jesus voluntarily died in my place to free me from the bondage of sin.
2. God can forgive sin.
3. Through God's powerful indwelling Holy Spirit, we are able to live righteously.

<u>**Prayer:**</u> Lord, accept my confession of sin. Help me to turn to you and step out in faith, seeking to please you in all I do. Guide me in, and through, your Word and show me how to live righteously for you. Help me to be attentive to the leading of the Holy Spirit and seek His guidance each day. Amen.

<u>**What is my response to God's promise?**</u>

What do I need to confess and ask forgiveness for today?

____

____

____

How is my life different because I am forgiven by God?

____

____

____

<u>**Promise Confirmation:**</u> Isaiah 53:4-6, Romans 1:16-17, Romans 5: 6-9, 2 Corinthians 5:21, Ephesians 3:16-19

Day 64

Can I Come In?

Revelation 3:20

"*Behold, I stand at the door and knock. If anyone hears my voice and opens the door, I will come in to him and eat with him, and he with me.*"

Promise: God promises Jesus will come in and abide with those who open their hearts' door and invite Him to enter.

When was the last time you expectantly opened the door of your home? It would depend, I'm sure, on who you thought was knocking. If it is a friend, you are put at ease by the sound of their voice and greeting. It makes one eager to open the door and receive friendship and warmth. Jesus wants to meet and greet us as His friend. He knows if we will let Him enter into our lives, we will respond to His voice and have joy in His company. Do you know this kind of fellowship with Him? Ask Him in today and be greeted by His loving voice.

Lessons and Truths:

1. God waits for my acceptance of Jesus as Savior to establish His relationship with me.

2.   Asking God to enter my life is essential to having the Holy Spirit indwell me.
3.   Jesus' presence brings fellowship, sharing, and response to His voice.

Prayer: Lord Jesus, I am so privileged to call you friend and know your voice. Help me to set aside time each day to fellowship with you, listen to your voice and study your Word. Give me a desire to know you better and trust you fully as my friend and Savior. Holy Spirit bring a fresh awareness of your indwelling Spirit today, that I may live with conviction and stand firmly for you. Amen.

What is my response to God's promise?

Jesus promises a relationship with those who listen to His voice and let Him enter into their lives. How would you describe your relationship with Jesus? ____________________________________

____

Do you know Jesus as Lord and Savior?_________*If not, see 1 John 1:9, Romans 10:9, and 8:9-11. Invite Him to dwell with you. Pray a simple prayer, confess your sin, profess your faith in the fact that Jesus died on the cross and rose from the dead to pay your sin debt. Ask Him to come into your life. You will then be free in Christ for eternity.*

If you know Christ as your Lord and Savior, who do you know that does not know Him? ____________________________
Pray for their salvation now.

Promise Confirmation: Psalm 91:9-16, Luke 11:9-13, John 17:20-26, Ephesians 1:13-14

<u>Day 65</u>

Unfailing Love and Peace

Isaiah 54:10

"Though the mountains be shaken and the hills be removed, yet my unfailing love for you will not be shaken nor my covenant of peace be removed,' says the LORD, who has compassion on you."

<u>Promise</u>: God promises that nothing can shake His love or remove His peace from me.

I live in earthquake country and have seen the devastation resulting from an earthquake. Literally, everything comes tumbling down and is leveled. There is nothing that can stop the destruction once the quake begins. God is promising me that *no matter what,* even the greatest disaster, will not stop Him from loving and caring for me. His peace can and will always be with me. God wants me to stay in His love and have access to His peace each and every day. Are you claiming His love and peace for your life? It is there for the asking.

<u>**Lessons and Truths:**</u>

1. God is tenacious with those He loves.
2. God will never abandon me.
3. God gives peace.
4. God is full of compassion toward me.
5. God's plans, love, compassion, and mercy are eternal.
6. No circumstance I face will ever be bigger than Almighty God.

<u>**Prayer:**</u> Lord, I am humbled by your love and compassion for me. No matter how many times I fail, you still love me. You are always with me in every circumstance and, tenaciously, hold onto me with your love. Cover me in your love and hold me tightly, so that I may walk each day with you. Amen.

<u>**What is my response to God's promise?**</u>

Where do I need God's peace to replace my worry?

____

____

____

Where do I need to trust God's love for me more fully? ______

____

____

____

<u>**Promise Confirmation:**</u> Deuteronomy 31:6, Psalm 62:1-2, 6-8, Lamentations 3:21-23, John 14:27, Romans 8:35-39, Philippians 4:6-7

<u>Day 66</u>

Perfect Fulfillment

Psalm 138:7-8a

"Though I walk in the midst of trouble, you preserve my life; you stretch out your hand against the anger of my foes, with your right hand you save me. The LORD will fulfill his purpose for me; your love, O LORD, endures forever."

Promise: God promises to preserve and save me, deal with my enemies, and fulfill His purpose for my life.

Stop for a minute and ponder the magnitude of this promise. The God of the universe, Creator all things, is promising to save me with His right hand. Jesus is the one who sits at the right hand of God in heaven. He was sent by God to save me and preserve me for all eternity. God also promises to avenge wrongs done to me and fulfill the purpose He has for my life. I have a purpose that is planned, preserved by God, and it will be completed. God's will cannot be thwarted. He does not change his mind. He has the best planned for me. I need to let this truth seep into my soul: God is always with me and wills the best for me. It is a blessed assurance that is wrapped in His love for eternity.

<u>Lessons and Truths</u>:
1. God walks with me at all times.
2. God preserves my life though my faith in Jesus—His right hand.
3. God will avenge wrongs done to me.
4. God has a purpose for the life of each believer.
5. God and His love are eternal.

<u>Prayer</u>: Lord, I am overwhelmed that you have a special purpose for me. You redeemed me through your love and constantly keep me in your care. Each day, I am preserved by your grace and support, as I deal with others. I want to be used mightily for your kingdom and trust you to fulfill your purpose for my life. Give me eyes to see what you want me to see, ears to hear what you want me to do or say. I want to glorify you. Amen.

<u>What is my response to God's promise?</u>

Do I have wrongs that I feel God needs to avenge? Submit them to God, and leave them with Him. _______________________

____

What do I see as God's purpose for my life right now? _______

____

____

Pray and seek alignment with God's will.

<u>Promise Confirmation</u>:   Psalm 119:49-50, Jeremiah 29:11, Romans 12:19, 2 Corinthians 5:5, Ephesians 1:11-14, Philippians 2:12-13, Hebrews 1:3

<u>Day 67</u>

Sovereign God

Daniel 2:19-22

"During the night the mystery was revealed to Daniel in a vision. Then Daniel praised the God of heaven and said: 'Praise be to the name of God for ever and ever; wisdom and power are his. He changes times and seasons; he sets up kings and deposes them. He gives wisdom to the wise and knowledge to the discerning. He reveals deep and hidden things; he knows what lies in darkness and light dwells in him.'"

<u>Promise</u>: God promises to be in charge (sovereign), give wisdom and discernment, as well as reveal deep and hidden things to me through His omniscience.

This promise gives me great comfort when I hear disturbing world news. God wants to assure us that no matter how bad things look, He is the one who allows events to unfold as they do. The Bible is full of examples of how God used people, and events, to mold the future for the benefit of his people. I need to trust that God is in control, just as He says He is, and leave the future to His design. Fretting about the world and world events accomplishes nothing. What I need to do is pray and give my concerns to Him. He is the one that has the power to guide and change events. Focusing on God will allow me to move forward and allow Him be in control just as He intended. He promises me wisdom, discernment, and knowledge of Him, His character, and His kingdom, which can only be known by a child of God, through His power.

Lessons and Truths:

1. God sets time and allows nations and governments to exist.
2. God is wise and the source of all wisdom.
3. God gives me wisdom and discernment.
4. God can and does reveal things to me.
5. God is light. He knows and understands evil.

Prayer: Lord, you are, indeed, sovereign and omniscient. Cause me to accept these truths of your character so that I can trust you fully and set aside worry about future events. You tell me that your ways are not my ways. Help me to accept and understand your ways, so that I can boldly move forward for you. I crave wisdom and knowledge of you. Give me a hunger for your Word and perseverance to study and learn more about you. Pull me close and hold me, so that our relationship will grow, deepen, and bring you glory. Amen.

What is my response to God's promise?

How am I allowing God's light to fill me and push out any darkness (doubts, fears, unbelief)? ________________________

What do I need to seek God's wisdom for today? ____________

____

Promise Confirmation: 2 Chronicles 20:6, Psalm 75:6-7, Matthew 11:25, Ephesians 1:7-10, 1 John 1: 5-7

<u>Day 68</u>

Guiding Revelations

Daniel 2:23

"*I thank and praise you, O God of my fathers: You have given me wisdom and power, you have made known to me what we asked of you, and you have made known to us the dream of the king.*"

<u>Promise</u>: God promises to give me wisdom and power and to reveal what I *need* to know for the future.

How often do I fret because I don't know something? I am undecided about what to do because I don't know the possible outcome. Daniel did not know what the future would hold, but knew that God was in control and had revealed to him what he needed to know in order to speak with the king. Just like Daniel, I need to trust in God and seek His wisdom and guidance, through His Word and prayer. God promises to reveal what I *need* to know. Trust in God is paramount to living for Him, which can only be achieved by obedience, filled with thankfulness and praise. Turn your questions to God, along with praise and thanksgiving, your mind and heart will be comforted as you trust in Him.

<u>Lessons and Truths</u>:
1. God is to be praised and thanked.
2. God gives wisdom to believers.
3. God gives power to do His work.
4. God can and does reveal what I *need* for my future.

<u>Prayer</u>: Lord, you are the one who knows all things and has the power to control the future. Give me patience as I wait upon you for answers to my prayers. Guide me in your ways and direct my path. Let my heart be filled with praise to you and trust in your sovereignty. Thank you for your goodness and the hope I have in you. Amen.

<u>What is my response to God's promise?</u>

How am I trusting God daily to provide and guide me?

____

____

____

What can I thank Him for right now? ___________________

____

____

<u>Promise Confirmation</u>: Proverbs 2:6, Acts 1:7-8, 1 Corinthians 2:9-13, Ephesians 3:9-12, 2 Peter 1:3-4

<u>Day 69</u>

Conquerors through Christ

Romans 8:35-37

"*Who shall separate us from the love of Christ? Shall trouble or hardship or persecution or famine or nakedness or danger or sword? As it is written: 'For your sake we face death all day long; we are considered as sheep to be slaughtered.' No, in all these things we are more than conquerors through him who loved us.*"

<u>**Promise:**</u> God promises us victory though Christ's love.

This verse gives us the blessed assurance that God's love for us, through Christ, is so strong that nothing can separate us from it. Paul cited troubles, persecution (for our faith), bodily deprivation, and war as obstacles that we may face. He said that none of those things will come between us and Christ's love. His love is eternal and we step into that love when we accept Jesus as our Savior. Are you in Christ's love today? Be sure He is your Savior before you even begin your day.

<u>**Lessons and Truths:**</u>

1. Once we accept Christ as Savior we are His eternally.
2. God is sovereign over all the heavens and earth.
3. Persecution and hardships are to be expected in the life of the believer.
4. God's love is stronger than anything we can ever face.
5. God's way leads to victory.

<u>Prayer:</u> Lord, you are the Creator of love and have made the bonds of Christ's love for me unbreakable. You know me and will keep me in your love for all eternity. Help me to show that kind of love to those I meet today and give me courage to face adversity, knowing Christ is always with me. I trust you for victory in my life and claim it in your name. Amen.

<u>What is my response to God's promise?</u>

Where is God giving me victory?______________________

____

____

Where do I need to claim victory and turn over battle to Him?

____

____

____

<u>Promise Confirmation:</u> Psalm 23, Psalm 138:7-8, 1 Corinthians 15:54-58, 2 Corinthians 12:9-10, 1 John 5:3-5

<u>Day 70</u>

Separation Impossible!

Romans 8:38-39

"*For I am convinced that neither death nor life, neither angels nor demons, neither present nor the future, nor any powers, neither height nor depth, nor anything else in all creation, will be able to separate us from the love of God that is in Christ Jesus our Lord.*"

<u>Promise</u>: God promises that nothing on earth, under the earth, in the heavens, in the present, in the future, not even in death, will be able separate us from Christ's love.

This is a powerful promise that encourages me and gives me hope when I am faced with adversity. Paul acknowledges that fear of the future, death, Satan's power and the world itself can cause us to doubt God's love. He assures us in this verse, that no matter what the circumstances, God's love is greater. Christ was victorious over death on the cross. He is higher than even the angels. Demons obey him, so what have I to fear in life if Christ is with me? Paul had many opportunities to see for himself the depth of Christ's love for him. He was convinced that he could not be separated from the love of Christ. Are you convinced?

Lessons and Truths:

1. Angels and demons are real.
2. God is sovereign over worldly powers and time.
3. Nothing in creation can stand in the way of God's love for me.
4. God's love is demonstrated through His provision of Christ to save me and restore my relationship with Him.

Prayer: Lord, you are sovereign over all of your creation. You are unchanging in character and so is your love for me. Thank you for sending Christ to die for my sins, so that I can come into a relationship with you, free of my sin. Your love upholds me as I face difficult circumstances each day. Use the challenges I encounter to build and mold my character, that I may glorify you and show your love to others. Amen.

What is your response to God's promise?

What are you trying to accomplish in your own power that you need to give to God? _______________________________

____

Who do you know in need of Christ as Savior? Pray for his or her salvation._______________________________

____

Promise Confirmation: Psalm 91: 9-12, Isaiah 25:8, Daniel 2:20-23, John 10:29-30, 2 Timothy 1:9-10, 1 John 4:13-16

Author's Note

I am so thankful for your diligence and commitment to study Scripture. God is faithful and I know He has blessed you through His Word. Now what? I arrived at lesson 70 and knew I was not yet done with this book. God laid on my heart ten extra days connected to some of my favorite promises. I know He chose these for me, and I pray that they will be an extra blessing to you. Each day is an expansion of a promise using the related Scriptures. God chose the related Scriptures and then allowed me to see a connection that I could apply to my life. Each application could result in changes that would dramatically affect my life, if I would be open and yielded to Him. I was amazed again at the depth of God's Word and how timely His ancient words are to our 21st century lives!

After I finished all the Days, I realized that it was time to go back and start again. This is a study that I will do countless times working to memorize the promises and learning to meditate on them each day. I pray that this has been a rich study for you and that you will not hesitate to do it again.

May the profound Word of God touch you anew each time you open His Word,

Linda Knight

<u>Day 71</u>

Victorious Living

Lamentations 3:21-23

"But this I call to mind, and therefore I have hope: The steadfast love of the LORD never ceases; his mercies never come to an end; they are new every morning; great is your faithfulness."

<u>Promise</u>: God promises His love and faithfulness will never end and His mercies are new each morning.

<u>Why is it important to know this promise?</u>

God's character is revealed: His steadfast (constant) Love, Mercy, Eternality, and Faithfulness.

This promise provides me with: hope, comfort, assurance of God's unfailing love, and a fresh outlook for each day.

<u>Looking at related promises:</u>

Jeremiah 29:11: *"For I know the plans I have for you, declares the LORD, plans for welfare and not for evil, to give you a future and a hope"*

Romans 8:38-39: *" For I am sure that neither death nor life, nor angles nor rulers, nor things present nor things to come, nor powers, nor height nor depth, nor anything else in all creation , will be able to separate us from the love of God in Christ Jesus our Lord."*

When you get up in the morning do you say: "Good morning, Lord!" or "LORD! It's morning!"? If I rise each day with a defeated attitude, I am saying the God I know cannot possibly tackle and defeat the things I am facing today. God wants me to live with hope and assurance that He is, indeed, sovereign over what I face each day. He has plans for me and my life and wants only good things for me. With Him, I can be more than a conqueror and live a victorious life. I have His promise that His mercies are new each morning. What am I afraid of then?

Prayer: Lord, I know that you have an infinitely better plan for my life than I could make on my own. Develop hope within me. Bind Satan and his attacks of depression, doubt, and fear. Have mercy upon me and cover me with your love. Hold me in your faithful hands as I begin each new day. Amen.

How can I use this promise?

Where did I see God's mercy yesterday? ___________________

____

Where do I need God's mercy today? ___________________

____

What fearful situation or person am I facing where I need God's help? ____

<u>Day 72</u>

Watchful Living

James 4:7-8a

"*Submit yourselves therefore to God. Resist the devil, and he will flee from you. Draw near to God, and he will draw near to you.*"

<u>Promise</u>: If I will *submit* (yield, obey) to God, *resist* (oppose, withstand) Satan, and *come near* (approach) to Him, He will come near to me and Satan will flee!

<u>Why is it important to know this promise?</u>

God's character is revealed: God loves obedience, God is greater than Satan, He is approachable and accessible.

This promise provides me with: direction in life, hope, confidence to resist Satan, assurance of Satan's departure and an assurance of my relationship with Almighty God.

<u>Looking at related promises:</u>

1 Samuel 15:22: "*And Samuel said, 'Has the LORD as great delight in burnt offerings and sacrifices, as in obeying the voice* *of the LORD? Behold, to obey is better than sacrifice, and to listen than the fat of rams.'"*

Hebrews 4:16: *"Let us then with confidence draw near to the throne of grace, that we may receive mercy and find grace to help in time of need."*

1 Peter 5:8-9: *"Be sober-minded; be watchful. Your adversary the devil prowls around like a roaring lion, seeking someone to devour. Resist him, firm in your faith, knowing that the same kinds of suffering are being experienced by your brotherhood throughout the world."*

As a culture we pride ourselves on our independence. We like to say, "I'm my own person!" Those attitudes are not in line with what the Lord desires for us. He loves for us to be obedient, confident, and watchful. God knows that His ways lead to what is good for us, lives filled with his grace and mercy, and a strong stance against the Devil. The key to obedience is drawing near to God, through our Lord Jesus Christ. He opens the way for us to have a sustaining relationship with God, which will fill our lives with His grace and mercy. Jesus will help us to stand firm in faith and not be turned aside by Satan. Hold fast to Jesus and you will be able to stand, obey, and draw near to God.

<u>Prayer</u>: Precious Jesus, in you I am able to stand and resist all the temptations that Satan places in my path. Help me to step over them or go around them, so that they will not deter me from following you and doing what you have for me to do. Keep me in your care, that I may be filled with your grace and mercy. Amen.

How can I use this promise?

Where do I need to submit to God's ways, instead of my own?

____

____

____

Where do I need to be watchful for Satan's attack? __________

____

____

____

<u>Day 73</u>

Word-Guided Living

Psalm 119:105

"Your word is a lamp to my feet and a light to my path."

<u>Promise</u>: God promises that His Word will provide light and guidance for my life.

<u>Why is it important that I know this promise?</u>

God's character is revealed: God's Word guides, His Word is true, He is Light, Truth, and our Omniscient Guide.

This promise provides me with: Truth for living, guidance and knowledge that God has designed a plan for my life.

<u>Looking at related promises:</u>

Proverbs 30:5 *"Every word of God proves true; he is a shield to those who take refuge in him."*

Hebrews 4:12   *"For the word of God is living and active, sharper than any two-edged sword, piercing to the division of* *soul and of spirit, of joints and of marrow, and discerning the thoughts and intentions of the heart."*

With His words God created the universe, He spoke it into existence. The power in the spoken and written Word of God is incomprehensible. Proverbs tells us the words are true and will always be proven true in every circumstance. The verse also adds that God can and does defend and protect us. Hebrews says that God's Word is living, active, and the ultimate weapon. Unlike any human weapon, the Word of God can penetrate and divide spiritual, as well as physical things. In light of these verses, I should not take God's Word lightly. I should read it to strengthen and build up my faith and increase my knowledge of Him. I should also treat it with reverence and honor, as unto God himself. It is comforting to know that I have such a powerful force, available at my fingertips, to guide and direct me each day. Read it, and feel God's power in your life!

Prayer: Lord, thank you that your Word is accessible to me each day. Open my eyes that I may take in your truth and mediate on your Word. Help me to hide your Word in my heart, use it to speak to others, and to give me strength and courage. Amen.

How can I use this promise?

Choose a few of the promises in this book and memorize them.

____

____

Where is God using His Word to speak to me? _______________

____

<u>Day 74</u>

Godly Living

Psalm 37:5-6

"*Commit your way to the LORD; trust in him, and he will act. He will bring forth your righteousness as the light, and your justice as the noonday.*"

<u>Promise</u>: God promises to act on my behalf, bring out righteousness and justice for me if I will commit myself to Him and trust Him.

<u>Why is it important to know this promise?</u>

God's character is revealed: He is Trustworthy, Righteous, Just, Faithful and Sovereign.

This promise provides me with: security, knowledge of His ability to change and mold my character, His righteousness, light and justice.

<u>Looking at related promises:</u>

Isaiah 30:18 *"Therefore the LORD waits to be gracious to you, and therefore he exalts himself to show mercy to you. For* *the LORD is a God of justice; blessed are all those who wait for him."*

Matthew 7:11 *"If you then, who are evil, know how to give good gifts to your children, how much more will your Father who is in heaven give good things to those who ask him!"*

What are the benefits of godly character? This verse tells us that committing to the Lord will cause God to act our behalf. Who better to have in our corner or on our side than the Lord Almighty? He will make us shine with righteousness and justice like the bright light of the sun. There is no way we can achieve this on our own, and as Romans 3:23 reminds us, *"For all have sinned and fall short of the glory of God."* Romans 3:24 continues, *"and are justified by his grace as a gift, through the redemption that is in Christ Jesus."* Through Jesus, God imparts His character to me and will cause me to shine for Him. What a wonderful gift from our heavenly Father!

Prayer: Lord, thank you for the good things you have for me through your Son, Jesus. Mold me and shape me into His image, that I may glorify you with my actions, motivated by your righteousness and justice. Cause my light to shine before my family, friends, and strangers. May they know that I belong to you. Amen.

How can I use this promise?

What godly character am I exhibiting in my life? __________

____

____

See Galatians 5:22-23 — the fruits of the Spirit.

What areas of my life do I need to commit more fully to the
Lord? ____

____

____

____

<u>Day 75</u>

Stress-Free Living

Philippians 4:19

"*And my God will supply every need of yours according to his riches in glory in Christ Jesus.*"

<u>Promise</u>: God promises to supply for my every need.

<u>Why is it important that I know this promise?</u>

God's character is revealed: God is the Ultimate Resource, He is Sovereign and Owner of all. He is my Omniscient Caring Provider.

This promise provides me with: assurance that God knows exactly what I need and will provide for me. God loves and cares about me and He is sovereign over all things that happen to me.

<u>Looking at related Promises:</u>

Psalm 34:9 "*Oh, fear the LORD, you his saints, for those who fear him have no lack.*"

Matthew 6:25-33: *Therefore I tell you, do not be anxious about your life, what you will eat or what you will drink, nor about your body, what you will put on. Is not life more than food, and the body more than clothing? Look at the birds of the air: they neither sow nor reap nor gather into barns, and yet your heavenly Father feeds them. Are you not more valuable than they? And which of you by being anxious can add a single hour to his span of life? And why are you anxious about clothing? Consider the lilies of the field, how they grow: they neither toil nor spin, yet I tell you, even Solomon in all his glory was not arrayed like one of these. But if God so clothes the grass of the field, which today is alive and tomorrow is thrown into the oven, will he not much more clothe you, O you of little faith? Therefore do not be anxious, saying, 'What shall we eat?' Or What shall we drink? 'or 'What shall we wear?' For the Gentiles seek after all these things, and your heavenly Father knows that you need them all. But seek first the kingdom of God and his righteousness, and all these things will be added to you.*

The twenty-first century is very materialistic, but from the above references, I see that people during King David's and Jesus' times worried about their basic needs, too. What to wear and what to eat are universal topics of concern then and now. All of these passages show that God is in control and knows our needs. He will provide for our care. The question is: why don't we trust God to do this? Why do we insist on worrying or grumbling? Jesus reminds us in the Matthew passage that we need to REST in the LORD. King David reminds us that fearing God will result in everything being taken care of. I think of all the time I waste worrying or complaining about money, furniture, clothes, cars, etc., when I know in my heart, it would be better spent worshiping, praising, reading the Word, talking to others about Jesus, and serving others instead! How about you? Can you trust God today for your needs and leave the rest in His hands?

Prayer: Lord, help me to rid my life of selfish pursuits and learn to focus on godly things. Give me opportunities to trust you and step out in faith. Open my eyes so that I can see these opportunities and praise you in faith. Grow my faith, so that I can live with the blessed assurance that you are, indeed, taking care of all of my needs, physically and spiritually. Amen.

How can I use this promise?

What am I worried or grumbling about that I need to give to the Lord? _______________________________________

____

____

____

<u>Day 76</u>

Confident Living

2 Corinthians 12:9-10

"But he said to me, 'My grace is sufficient for you, for my power is made perfect in weakness.' Therefore I will boast all the more gladly of my weaknesses, so that the power of Christ may rest upon me. For the sake of Christ, then, 'I am content with weaknesses, insult, hardship, persecutions, and calamities. For when I am weak, then I am strong.'"

<u>Promise</u>: God promises that His grace is sufficient, and He can use me, even though I am imperfect and weak.

<u>Why is it important that I know this promise?</u>

God's character is revealed: He is Sovereign, Omnipotent, Perfect, Omniscient, and Jehovah Jireh—the God who is Enough, the God who Provides.

This promise provides me with: assurance that He will give me what I need by His grace no matter what the circumstances, and I can rely on His strength and provision.

<u>**Looking at related promises:**</u>

1 Corinthians 1:25 *"For the foolishness of God is wiser than men, and the weakness of God is stronger than men."*

Ephesians 2:8-10 *"For by grace you have been saved through faith. And this is not your own doing; it is the gift of God, not a result of works, so that on one may boast. For we are his workmanship, created in Christ Jesus for good works, which God prepared beforehand, that we should walk in them.*

Hebrews 4:16 *"Let us then with confidence draw near to the throne of grace, that we many receive mercy and find grace to help in time of need."*

These verses reveal the amazing mercy of our God. He uses us to do His work and has created us anew in, and through, Christ Jesus. He has created a pathway of life and work for us to do. We can access His infinite grace and mercy by drawing near to Him, through His Word and in prayer. The Holy Spirit indwells each believer and gives us His power. He assures us that the power within us is greater than anything we can ever face. Without the power of the Holy Spirt, we are powerless, but by God's grace we can access His power and be more than victorious now and for eternity! As Paul said, *"For when I am weak, then I am strong."* Praise God for His glorious grace!

<u>**Prayer:**</u> Lord, you are all the sufficiency that I will ever need. You make me whole and complete, perfect in your sight though Jesus. Thank you. Increase my faith so that I will learn to trust you more deeply for the hard things in life and claim your grace

and mercy over my thoughts and actions. I desire to glorify you
in all I say and do. Amen.

How can I use this promise?

Where do I need God's grace in my life? ___________________

____

____

____

____

<u>Day 77</u>

Trust-Filled Living

Jeremiah 29:11

"'*For I know the plans I have for you,' declares the LORD, 'plans to prosper you and not to harm you, plans to give you hope and a future.'*"

<u>Promise</u>: God promises His plans for my life are good and filled with hope.

<u>Why is it important to know this promise?</u>

God's character is revealed: His Sovereignty, Omniscience, Goodness and Caring.

Promise provides me with: hope, assurance of His care, an assured future, and His direction and guidance in my life.

<u>Looking at related promises:</u>

Psalm 40:4-5 "*Blessed is the man who makes the LORD his trust, who does not look to the proud, to those who turn aside to false gods. Many, O LORD my God, are the wonders you have done. The things you planned for us no one can recount to you;*"

were I to speak and tell of them, they would be too many to declare."

Lamentations 3:25-26 *"The LORD is good to those whose hope is in him, to the one who seeks him; it is good to wait quietly for the salvation of the LORD."*

Matthew 7:11 *"If you, then, though you are evil, know how to give good gifts to your children, how much more will your Father in heaven give good gifts to those who ask him!"*

Pondering the above verses, I realize that HOPE is an essential product of faith. God wants me to live blessed by Him, awaiting the things He has planned for me, and living with an expectation that God's provision will be good. Lamentations reminds us that the LORD is good. It is part of His character to be good in all things, and anything He makes *is* good. Jesus tells us that only good gifts come from God, the Father. Once I have received God's best gift—Jesus, I am open to receive the many good gifts He has in store for me. Salvation, eternity, hope, care, unfailing love and peace are just a few of God's gifts to me though faith. Psalm 40:4 says it perfectly: *"Blessed is the man who makes the LORD his trust."*

<u>Prayer:</u> Lord, I know that you love and care for me. You have my best interest at heart and have fulfilling plans for my life. Help me to walk in your ways and seek you. Give me a desire for your good gifts and the patience to wait for your timing. I praise and thank you for your goodness and the hope you give me through Jesus. Amen.

<u>**How can I use this promise?**</u>

Where am I placing my trust (in things and people of this world or in God)? ______________________________________

____

____

____

Am I afraid of God's plans? ___________ If so, why?

____

____

____

____

What steps do I need to take to stay within God's plans? _____

____

____

____

Day 78

Resourceful Living

Hebrews 13:5-8

"*Keep your lives free from the love of money and be content with what you have, because God has said, 'Never will I leave you; never will I forsake you,' So we say with confidence, 'The Lord is my helper; I will not be afraid. What can man do to me?' Remember your leaders, who spoke the word of God to you. Consider the outcome of their way of life and imitate their faith. Jesus Christ is the same yesterday and today and forever.*"

Promise: God will NEVER leave me or abandon me. He will help me and keep me from being afraid, and God is unchanging for all eternity.

Why is it important to know this promise?

God's character is revealed: He is Immutable, Provider, Faithful, Helper, Protector, Peace, Redeemer, Omnipresent and Sovereign Lord.

This promise provides me with: contentment, hope, safety, peace of mind and soul, and a Foundational Rock (Jesus

Christ) upon which I can build my life.

<u>Looking at related promises:</u>

Psalm 46:1-3 *"God is our refuge and strength, an ever-present help in trouble. Therefore we will not fear, though the earth give way and the mountains fall into the heart of the sea, though its waters roar and foam and the mountains quake with their surging."*

Matthew 28: 19-20 *"Therefore go and make disciples of all nations, baptizing them in the name of the Father and of the Son and of the Holy Spirit, and teaching them to obey everything I have commanded you. And surely I am with you always, to the very end of the age."*

James 1:17 *"Every good gift and perfect gift is from above, coming down from the Father of the heavenly lights, who does not change like shifting shadows."*

Have you considered your resources for living? God assures us that He is our refuge and strength. He is with us 24/7, will dispel our fears, gives *only good gifts*, does not change and will be present with us for eternity. Wow! What a list of provisions! They are all based on our faith and trust in God. There is nothing that can be bought or earned. God is not whimsical and will not change His mind about loving and caring for us. Although the world is crashing all around us, we can live with confidence that God will provide and will always be present with us. These are powerful resources for the faithful.

Prayer: Lord, you are so good and provide me with exactly what I need. I can count on your presence and peace in my life, thank you. Cause me to grow in faith and walk trusting in your provision. Open my eyes to see your good and perfect gifts as they come into my life. Use me to do your good works, so that I may glorify you. Amen.

How can I use this promise?

Where do I need to trust God today? ____________________

____

____

____

____

<u>Day 79</u>

Redeemed Living

1 Peter 2:24

"*He himself bore our sins in his body on the tree, that we might die to sin and live to righteousness. By his wounds you have been healed.*"

<u>Promise</u>: God promises that through Jesus' death on the cross my sins are forgiven, and I can live a righteous life in Him.

<u>Why is it important to know this promise?</u>

God's character is revealed: He is Redeemer, Forgiver of sin, Righteous and Healer.

This Promise provides me with: salvation, healing, freedom from the power of sin, freedom from guilt, ability to live righteously, and the indwelling Holy Spirit.

<u>Looking at related promises:</u>

Romans 5:6-9 "*For while we were still weak, at the right time Christ died for the ungodly. For one will scarcely die for a righteous person—through perhaps for a good person one would* *dare even to die—but God shows his love for us in that while we were still sinners, Christ died for us. Since, therefore, we have now been justified by his blood, much more shall we be save by him from the wrath of God.*

2 Corinthians 5:21 *"For our sake he made him to be sin who knew no sin, so that in him we might become the righteousness of God.*

Paul rightly argues that we will not willingly die for someone else, especially if that person is not nice. It is beyond comprehension that God loved us so much, He provided Jesus to take the penalty for our sins and make us clean. God desires a relationship with us that can only be achieved if we are made clean. God is holy and pure and cannot abide with sin. We are redeemed and made right with God though the sacrifice Jesus made on the cross. He took God's wrath over our sin and made atonement for us. What a wonderful redeemer we have! In 1 Peter 2:24, it says we are healed by his wounds. Yes, he bled and died so that we might live now and eternally with Him. Thank you Lord Jesus.

<u>Prayer</u>: Lord, I confess that I am a sinner, saved by your grace though the blood of Jesus. Thank you for providing a way for me to be clean and holy before you. I cannot imagine the pain you felt at your Son's death, and I am humbled and awed that He gave His life for me. I know you love me and desire me to live righteously. Give me the strength, through your indwelling Holy Spirit, to live righteously and glorify you each day. Amen.

<u>**How can I use this promise?**</u>

How has Jesus healed me? _______________________________

____

____

Who do I know that does not know Jesus?_________________

____

____

Pray for their salvation.

Day 80

Prayer-Filled Living

John 14:27

"Peace I leave with you; my peace I give you. I do not give to you as the world gives. Do not let your hearts be troubled and do not be afraid."

Promise: God promises His peace, which will leave my heart untroubled and unafraid.

Why is it important to know this promise?

God's character is revealed: His Peace, Care for His creation and Sovereignty. He is Omnipotent (All-Powerful), Omnipresent (Ever-Present) and Omniscient (All-Knowing).

This promise provides me with: peace, comfort, freedom from fear, and hope.

Looking at related promises:

Psalm 29:11 *"The LORD gives strength to his people; the LORD blesses his people with peace.*

Isaiah 26:3-4 *"You will keep in perfect peace him whose mind is steadfast, because he trusts in you. Trust in the LORD forever, for the LORD, the LORD, is the Rock eternal.*

John 16:33 *"I have told you these things, so that in me you may have peace. In this world you will have trouble. But take heart! I have overcome the world."*

Philippians 4:6-7 *"Do not be anxious about anything, but in everything, by prayer and petition, with thanksgiving, present your requests to God. And the peace of God, which transcends all understanding, will guard your hearts and your minds in Christ Jesus."*

Why is it that we crave peace in our lives? These verses give us clues into our source of worry. We are weak and at the mercy of the world. Without God and His indwelling Holy Spirit, we are open to Satan's attacks. Our minds are prone to wander and lose heart if we are not grounded in the Lord. The world is swirling around us and, at times, it seems like it will overwhelm us. Jesus, then later Paul, offered us insight on how we can keep peace in our lives: Pray, pray, pray, be thankful, and focus our hearts on Jesus! It seems simple enough to say, but very hard to do! But Jesus promised He is greater than the world, and we will be victorious in and through Him!

<u>**Prayer:**</u> Lord, I crave your peace in my life. Give me a heart overflowing with gratitude and thankfulness. Open my eyes to see troubling situations through *your* eyes and place my full trust in you. Dispel my fears and give me an attitude of peacefulness,

to live each day glorifying you. Amen.

<u>How can I use this promise?</u>

Name those things that are causing fear in your life, and then claim victory over them in Jesus name.

____

____

____

____

____

How much time do I spend in prayer each day?____________

How can I increase this? ______________________________

____

____

____